ZERO LOST REVENUE DAYS

REVENUE DAYS

A REVOLUTIONARY APPROACH TO SELLING
SENIORS HOUSING & HEALTHCARE

TRACI BILD

A REVOLUTIONARY APPROACH TO SELLING
SENIORS HOUSING & HEALTHCARE

ZERO LOST REVENUE DAYS

TRACI BILD

ZERO LOST REVENUE DAYS A Revolutionary Approach to
Selling Seniors Housing and Healthcare

Traci Bild Enterprises

Copyright © 2015 by Traci Bild

All Rights Reserved

Published in the United States by Traci Bild Enterprises, a division of Dynamic
Performance International, Inc. Tampa, Florida.

www.BildandCo.com

Cover design by Studio Max
Book design by Sue Balcer

Cataloging-in-Publication Data is on file
with the Library of Congress.

2nd Edition
ISBN 978-0-9964846-1-9

PRINTED IN THE UNITED STATES OF AMERICA

Dedicated to two very special people who
paved my way in this amazing industry.

Debra DeRolf

Debra, you called and I answered, never realizing that my life would be forever changed. Because of you, I found my business soul mate—the Senior housing industry—and I will forever be grateful to you.

Jayne Sallerson

Jayne, I first heard the term Zero Lost Revenue Days from you and it stuck in my mind like crazy glue! Your quest for greatness (and fun) has always inspired me. Thanks for the introduction to a term that will be the blueprint for organizations looking to reach the pinnacle of success within our industry.

Table of Contents

ACKNOWLEDGEMENTS

I will never forget the first time I was introduced to the senior housing industry. I was on a business trip when I received a telephone call from my office manager, Brittney (who also happens to be my amazing mother). She said that a woman by the name of Debra DeRolf had called. Debra had picked up my first book, *7 Steps to Successful Selling* (Perigee 2001), at an airport bookstore and loved the simplicity of my message, and wanted to know if I could conduct some kind of training for her organization, The Fountains Retirement Communities. Never one to say no to a training opportunity, I said yes!

Let me start by saying that I knew nothing about senior housing. My immediate thought (like many of your prospects think) was "nursing homes." Upon talking to Debra, we decided that I would conduct a series of teleseminars for her organization. She then invited me to speak at several regional sales conferences and, ultimately, her national sales conference. I was not familiar with the industry, but I was a sales expert and knew that one golden truth applied: *relationships rule*. This industry, like so many others that I have worked in, was the same. The fact is, people buy people. I applied my sales systems and did my best to customize them to The Fountains. To better educate myself, I conducted many telephone and on-site mystery shops, had sales counselors record their incoming and outbound sales calls and forward them to me for review, and asked lots of questions.

By the end of the first year of working together, we grew The Fountains Retirement Communities' sales by over $4 million dollars. Debra was invited by Tony Mullen to speak at his annual Sales & Marketing Summit in Tampa to share her success, and she in turn invited me because it was my system that she felt had fueled their results. Since I lived in Tampa, I said yes and the rest, my friend, is history. I had no idea what I was getting into or how that two-hour presentation would forever change my life.

Many of my first clients—whom I now consider dear friends—were sitting in that very room.

The Tampa conference was the first time I met Jayne Sallerson as well. I will never forget it because the presentations were running long and they were a bit long-winded (it had been a long day). Then Jayne took the stage and immediately captured my attention; she spoke my language, she had the same energy level, and I simply had to meet her. From what Jayne says, she felt the same and since then I have had the opportunity to work with Jayne in many capacities and continue to learn from her to this day.

I want to take this opportunity to formally thank you, Debra, for picking up my first book, reading it, and calling my office to see if I could further assist you in growing occupancy. Your actions have not only forever changed my life, but thousands of sales counselors' lives, executive directors' lives, and the lives of those seniors who were impacted because these very people took action on what I taught them. Because of you, hundreds of providers have increased their occupancy and revenue, some to record levels, and in turn have expanded their portfolios, allowing them to reach more people. This is an instance where one phone call literally resulted in thousands of transformed lives. Thank you.

Thank you, Jayne, for believing in, mentoring, and introducing me to concepts specific to our industry, that when integrated with my training systems, exponentially drove results.

Thank you to all of my first clients, those who took a chance when I was literally the "new kid" on the block. You allowed me to dive into your organizations, implement aggressive training systems, tweak them, measure their effectiveness, and share the results in a way that will forever transform our industry.

I want to thank my amazing team here at Bild & Company. Wow, I am so incredibly blessed and could not have written this book without each and every one of you. Thanks for all you have done and will do for our organization. Your commitment to implementing our systems, no matter how difficult or challenging the community, is incredibly inspiring. Because of your desire to better our very best, our training has been taken to an entirely new level.

I want to thank my husband David for his continued support of my hopes, goals, and dreams. He is always standing tall by my side, encouraging me to do that which I'm not even sure I can do!

Last, but not least, I want to thank you for picking this book up and giving it a good read. I still have much work to do, but this book is something I am very proud of and it literally is just the beginning of many things we have in store for our amazing industry!

FOREWORD

I was one year into my role as Vice President of Sales & Marketing for a midsize senior living company when I first encountered Traci Bild and her sales systems. After years of testing several sales methods and programs, I continued to struggle with two challenges: training methods that were either too complicated or not scalable for employee turnover, and company growth. When I conducted sales training, my participants tended to get confused with which "step" they were on and which questions went with what step. The overall impact of these training sessions was nominal because after the training, many sales representatives focused on what step they were on instead of connecting with the customer. I was frustrated because I knew this didn't have to be so hard—it's not, after all, rocket science. I just needed something simple, organized, and easy to manage. I knew that anything I initiated in the company had to be scalable, cost effective, and most importantly, must make an occupancy impact.

As the company began to grow through acquisitions at an exponential rate, I knew I needed something different—fast. I talked to several of my mentors in the industry, but I found that everyone was using programs or systems that I already knew just did not work.

Then one day, I happened to be speaking at a sales and

marketing conference for the senior housing industry in Tampa, and decided to attend Traci Bild's presentation. As I sat in the audience, I expected this to be just another typical sales presentation. Within ten minutes of Traci's opening, I was blown away—someone finally got it! Traci's sales systems were exactly what I needed. Even though I didn't yet have every detail, I knew I had to take her program and run with it. I couldn't wait until her presentation was over so we could talk.

Within one month, I asked Traci to roll out her training systems to one region of my company so that I could test it. I saw results in the first thirty days. My sales staff was asking better, and more impactful, questions so they could better connect with the customers. My regional sales team could manage their sales more effectively because everyone in that region was using the same system and processes. Sales conversion rates went up, average move-ins went up, and occupancy went up. Needless to say, I rolled out the Traci Bild System company-wide and used it as a foundation for all of our sales training.

A year later I arranged for a keynote speaker to present at my annual sales meeting. He asked permission to "mystery shop" several of our communities and our competitors via telephone to use with his presentation. Within the week, he called me and said he was amazed at how consistent our communities were during the initial phone calls. Not only that, but he felt the questions we asked were especially impactful. As soon as I heard his comments, I knew I had a winning system in full force at all of our communities.

It is now eight years later, and I continue to be influenced by Traci in some form or fashion. I continue to use Traci's systematic approach as our sales foundation and I am amazed at how Traci enhances her methods, tools, and systems, making them more effective all the time. And of course, now with technology and the Internet, Traci engages us in new ways with tools such as her online podcasts, videocasts, blogging, and sales tips.

The senior housing industry has evolved substantially over the past ten years and the competition is fierce. Customers are willing to shop five or six communities before making a decision. In the mid-nineties, most companies hired sales staff based on personality rather than skill. Today, it takes skill and strategy.

I recently asked Traci and her coaching team to work with a select group of communities within our organization. With her help, our occupancy grew by 7.4% in just four months, and this was during the worst economic crisis we've seen since I entered the business. I have been an advocate of Traci's over the years because I know through experience that her sales process works. I know that the Traci Bild System is the answer.

—Jayne Sallerson
Senior Vice President, Emeritus Senior Living

Note to Reader: Second Edition update—Jayne Sallerson is now COO at Sherpa and Emeritus Senior Living, merged with Brookdale Senior Living, at the time of this printing.

CHAPTER ONE

INTRODUCTION

What's the date today? I want you to picture yourself exactly one year from today. How old will you be? Will you be living in the same house, the same city, or even the same state? What about your job? Will you still be operating, managing, or selling the senior living community where you are today? Will your occupancy and revenue be less or more? Will you be stressed out and on the verge of collapse, or will you be relaxed and confident due to strong occupancy performance? If only you had a crystal ball!

A decade ago, just about anyone could sell senior housing: build it and they would come! Alas, the days when you were the only provider in a five-mile radius are long gone. Today, there seem to be at least three to four competitors within three miles—all competing for the same new resident. Out of desperation, competitors offer deep discounts with the hope of winning the sale. Add in the advantages of a new property with all the bells and whistles, compared to an older, dated community, and it becomes even more difficult to achieve zero lost revenue days. Oh, and did I mention attrition? I've been in the industry for almost two decades and I've never seen it so high. Move ten in and lose twelve, for a net negative of two!

That can be very frustrating and emotionally draining.

The good news is that there is a pent-up demand and we have begun to see an influx of new prospects. The question to ask is, "How do I help them to see the value in moving to *my* community versus my competitors' and how do I get people to move now, not later?" It seems that you are up against quite a few obstacles, doesn't it?

We all know that the economy has gone through some dramatic upheavals in the last decade. Although we have seen recovery in both the stock and housing markets (at the time of publishing), we have not seen the recovery of the younger resident that we so covet. In truth, independent living has become the assisted living of yesterday, and assisted living has become the skilled nursing of yesterday. So much change!

It's safe to say we've entered a new era of selling senior housing. Today, it takes a skilled sales professional who has invested time in learning how to sell to a well-educated consumer. The difference between a pro and a novice is literally hundreds of thousands in increased revenue. If you are a member of management, training and education must be top of mind for your sales counselors. This book offers a great start.

I think it's safe to say that none of us ever imagined our economy would collapse like it did during the 2007-2009 calendar years. There were people who predicted it would happen, and most of us knew the housing bubble would burst, yet no one could guess the extent of the damage that would be done. I'll never forget how disconcerting it was to realize that our government had no clue as to what to do, and the sense that we'd truly entered uncharted territory.

Today, unemployment is back to 5.5% (at the time of this

writing, 2015) and we are in full recovery mode. Home values have recovered, the stock market has rebounded, and our industry, senior housing, wound up being a star. Outshining other real estate investments, the result for us has been a huge interest and investment in senior housing and care, which is incredibly exciting. While the Great Recession was an incredibly difficult time for our industry, it's proven to be a blessing in disguise. Now it's time to improve your game, to outperform your competitors, and enter a class of your own—with a focus on 100% occupancy and zero lost revenue days, along with rental fee integrity and the delivery of stellar care.

MAKE A DECISION

When the economy first started to decline, I made a commitment to myself. While many were bracing for the worst by cutting training budgets, laying off employees, and more, I made a conscious decision to invest more time, energy, and financial resources into my business than ever. I told myself that I would double my business and that nothing, not even a devastated economy, would stop me.

I had no idea if I would accomplish my goal or not, but in my mind nothing would stop me. What I did know is that I was not going to become complacent or begin to make excuses as to why business was slow. I have always told my clients that sales should not fluctuate depending on the weather, time of year, or outside factors. As sales professionals, the level of success we have is up to us. If the weather is horrible and no one will come out to meet you and visit your property, you should be delivering homemade soup and doing home visits instead. Getting to know people in their homes is an excellent opportunity to build relationships and really understand the situation that your prospect is in. Yet how many people actually do this? Isn't it easier to just make excuses and WAIT for the weather to get better, or for the holidays to pass? Not for me! I've always believed that success is in our own hands. If you want it badly enough, you will find a way—not wait for one to present itself.

That's what *Zero Lost Revenue Days* is all about. It is the pinnacle of success in our industry: zero days of lost revenue. Clearly, to do this you must have a strong team, a solid brand, thriving residents, and incredible care. Since you are going to show up to work every day anyway, why not show up screaming, "Success!" Trust me, it's much more fun to be at the top of your game than in the middle or at the bottom. The systems outlined in this book will provide you with the tools needed to make this vision a reality.

Back to that crystal ball—I see you at the peak of success. You are focused on growing sales and revenue to record levels. You have a strong, collaborative team environment, not just satisfied—but very satisfied—residents who regularly refer others to you, and professional referral sources who sing your praises. Even better, you spend half of what you used to on marketing expenditures due to referrals from residents, family, and professionals in the community, and you finally get that it's not about how much traffic you have but what you do with that traffic when you get it! In short, every lead is fully maximized, with no more waste.

Your competitors are in a state of awe, trying to figure out what in the world is going on. Your building is not the best by far, your services are not too different from theirs, and your prices are even a bit higher. Secretly, you enjoy being the envy of so many and realize that it wasn't luck that got you to this point—it was "preparation meeting opportunity." You had invested quality time in honing your skills, sharpening your saw; in fact, you went on a mission to become the Michelangelo of selling! It was a tough year of learning and discomfort, but the results were real and the evidence was concrete: solid systems yield results!

Okay, it's time to come back to reality. I know it's tempting to stay there in that comfortable future vision. Don't worry, that vision will become a reality soon enough. All you have to do is apply the information you are about to learn one day, one week, one month at a time. Before you know it, you won't just have a passion for the work you do but you'll have the skills needed to make a difference and get the move-ins or sales needed to start changing peoples' lives at an unprecedented level.

Before getting started, I would like to share what you can expect. The objective of this book is to help you learn to work smart, not hard, so you can work less, yet produce more than ever before. The end result? Increased revenue, a happy boss, and thrilled investors who will use that money to improve services, add more communities, and of course, there's a bonus for you: the more successful you are, the more leverage and job security you have. Think about it. No one will want to lose you, ever, if you make yourself invaluable. The very best part? Seniors whose lives will be forever changed because of YOU!

SELLING SYSTEMS

In order to work smart, not hard, you must have systems in place. The top 5% of all sales professionals who sell senior housing services understand that sales is a science and that the science must be followed in a precise order for it to be successful. How many units can a top sales professional in this industry sell?

The answer is, ten or more a month. The next tier, considered good salespeople, but not the best, sell six or more a month, and the average salespeople sell four a month. Odds are, if you have your hands on this material, you won't settle for being average—and in truth, with attrition, your community won't survive. You *must* seek to be the best. Let's get started. Here is what you are about to learn:

1. How to create a sales-driven culture

2. How to eliminate mismanaged calls and save $60,000+ a year

3. How to re-invent the inquiry process and convert 75% of all inquiries into an on-site visit

4. How to revolutionize tours and create a memorable personal experience

5. How to fuel follow-up and cut the sales cycle in half

6. How to close those hot but very challenging leads sitting on your desk

7. How to drive occupancy and revenue to record levels

Each system is easy to implement, simple to use, and revenue-driven. The hard part? Changing your habits. As a mother of two, I have found children to be much easier to train than adults. I can change the habits of a six-month-old or a three-year-old in a week. But an adult? I need four months or more!

Whoever said it takes just thirty days to change a habit is wrong. If you want long-term (not temporary) success, it takes a considerable amount of time and discipline.

My organization, Bild & Company, trains and coaches hundreds of employees from senior housing communities each week. The fact is, without accountability, very few people will follow through even if they really want to; life is just too hectic! But so much is at stake here, the most important of which is a tremendously better quality of life. I cannot stress how important it is for you to focus on these systems daily and not give up.

A MESSAGE TO THE LEADERS IN OUR INDUSTRY

If you are leading an organization that provides senior housing services and healthcare, I want to give you a few pointers to better maximize the concepts in this book, and the impact on your organization. I realize that you personally may not be involved in the day-to-day selling, yet you must lead by example. It's important that you have a clear understanding of our benchmarks, the new terminology set forth in this book, and the standards you must hold your sales counselors to.

Someone who I have always admired is Herb Keller of Southwest Airlines. A hands-on leader, he was known to show up on flights, at the ticket counter, and other "places" where executives in his position would never dare to go. Hands-on leadership made Southwest Airlines into one of the most successful airlines in history. Herb's strong leadership created an army of people who were eager to follow. He was never afraid to roll up his sleeves and get dirty. This garnered him immense respect from his employees and fueled their desire to perform at the highest standards.

When was the last time you showed up at a community and shadowed a tour? What about calling one personally to do a mystery shop and see what kind of service the prospects are receiving? I imagine if you've not done this, you either assume everything is going incredibly well and there is no need to waste your time, *or* you are terrified of what you might find and so are pretending everything is okay.

If that is the case, then *consider this your wake-up call.* Everything is not okay! The level of service being provided by our communities (as an industry) to prospective residents and their families is nowhere near where it should be. Sales counselors are acting as marketing directors—they are MARKETING, not selling or counseling people on the value the community offers. Instead of finding needs and building value, they are rambling off prices, pre-qualifying, listing every service known to man, and failing to find out anything about the prospect they are speaking with. Very rarely do we conduct a mystery shop and find otherwise. Don't believe me? Stop right now, pick up the phone, and randomly shop one of your communities.

To *do* better, people must *know* better. As the leader of your community or organization, it's up to you to provide the tools needed to succeed. The reason my company doubled in revenue each year during the recession and landed on *Inc.* magazine's "Fastest Growing Companies" list is that I read more, attended more seminars, and did everything I could to offset the impact the economic decline would have on my business. Knowledge is power!

WHAT'S NEXT?

As you read this book, highlight the areas that stand out to you as important to address within your organization. Use a pen and jot down ideas, thoughts, and action steps. You don't have to roll out every single system as outlined in this book, but pick a few that you feel would most impact occupancy and revenue, and start using them. Make it a point to be more hands-on when it comes to sales and raise the bar on sales expectations. I am asking you to be fully engaged. Our industry has been reshaped by the economic collapse. Giants we knew and admired are no longer here. There is tremendous opportunity for new leaders, innovators, and companies that are committed to the art of selling.

Partner with me—I have made it my mission to transform the way our services are offered to prospective residents and their family members. When people call on us in their time of need, it should be a memorable experience when individuals sense that they really matter. To change the experience people have when considering our services, we have to first change the mindset of those responsible for selling to them. To bring change to sales counselors, it must begin with the executive director. To transform the executive director, it must begin with the regional VP of sales or the owner(s) that they report to.

Your decision to read this book will not only impact your sales, revenue, and the efficiency of your sales department and community as a whole, but most importantly, the seniors we serve every single day. The better job we do, the better experience they will have, and that is what this is all about. Although I am teaching sales, it's really about learning the art of relationships. Sounds simple enough...yet it's just not happening. That must and will change—today is a new beginning!

CHAPTER TWO

THE MISMANAGED CALL CHALLENGE

MISMANAGED CALLS: FOOD FOR THOUGHT!

The results of a mystery shop study done by Dr. Margaret Wylde and David Smith, confirming those already done by Nowell and Rexhausen, showed the following:

- ❏ Many new inquiries or leads may be missed at all communities, but particularly those open for two years or more. Few communities reliably captured information about prospects, offered to send information, or invited them to visit the community.

- ❏ On average, the receptionists asked for the caller's name only 19% of the time.

- ❏ Approximately 60% of the sales counselors offered to send information to the prospect, while only 38% invited the prospect to visit.

- ❏ The receptionist transferred the shopper to another extension 68% of the time, offered to help 19% of the time, asked the caller to call back on 11% of the calls, and offered to take a message 1.4% of the time.

❑ The person answering the phone was the individual who offered to provide the information to the shopper 19.5% of the time.

❑ Shoppers did not talk to anyone who addressed their questions during their first call to the community a whopping 28.7% of the time.

Something very interesting that this study revealed is that both the receptionists and sales counselors at "full" communities (those with occupancies at 98% or more), appeared to stop making relevant inquiries to engage in selling. Indeed, both the telephone receptionists and sales staff among those full communities were often rude, missed appointments for the on-site visits, and/or kept the on-site shoppers waiting.

Our own research has confirmed that these facts are quite true. Of the mystery shops we have done to date, a minimum of 40% are mishandled, and oftentimes that number is actually higher (particularly at night and on weekends). For instance, we randomly shopped an industry leader and, out of five communities, we were not able to speak to even one sales counselor. Not one! We were asked to leave a message, call back, or accept the little bit of information the receptionist could give. With the competitive state of the industry and the poor media image, this is unacceptable.

Think this was a rare-case scenario? Here's a challenge for you: stop right now, pick up the phone, and call one of your company's communities. And don't stop there–call your competitors, too. You see, this is a universal problem. Organizations are dumping thousands of dollars into marketing in an effort to get leads, but when a lead literally falls out of the sky by calling in, there's no one available who is equipped to assist the inquirer! How insane is that?

MISMANAGED CALLS—WHAT ARE THEY?

Our definition of a mismanaged call is simply this:

A call from a prospective resident (or family member) who is seeking to learn more about your services, at which time one or more of the following occurs:

1. No one is immediately available who is qualified to take the call and answer the caller's questions;

2. The prospect is directed to voice mail or asked to leave a message;

3. No lead information is collected.

A mismanaged call will nearly always result in a lost lead.

HOW MANY CALLS ARE MISMANAGED?

Most companies have no idea how much money they are losing as a result of mismanaged calls. This is an epidemic in our industry. You can pick up the phone any time, any day of the week or weekend, and find that at minimum, 40% of the time no one will be available to assist you. Weekends are absolutely devastating. Give it a try right now.

HOW MUCH IS THIS COSTING YOU?

It depends on how you look at it. On average a lead calling in, at minimum, is costing you $500. I attended a recent conference where the number given was actually $800 per lead. Let's say you have ten solid inquiries a week that are coming into your community, due to the investment in marketing and referral outreach, and four are mismanaged—that equates to $2,000 per week at minimum, or upwards of $100,000 per year, per community! Do I have your attention yet?

The other way you can and should look at this is as a potential loss. Every time an inquirer calls, you have the potential to capture $40,000 or more annually as a result of a move-in. This is revenue left on the table. In our industry, people don't just call for fun. There is a driving reason, something has happened, and they need to learn more about how you can be of service to them. It's basically a 911 call!

WHAT'S THE SOLUTION?

My solution, which is proven to reduce mismanaged calls to 10% or less, is the following: *everyone must be involved in the sales process.* Sales counselors can't be all things to all people. They must go to the restroom, sleep, eat, conduct personal visits, and more. When they are doing these things, others must be available to provide the same level of service as the sales counselor. This is true whether it's the executive director, chef, activities director, or director of nursing. Sound difficult? It is... yet with our system, it's much, much easier.

Here is our system for eliminating mismanaged calls:

1. Create a sales-centered culture where the customer is the priority.

2. Create a hierarchy that is three-deep for each day of the week, during the day, *and* fully train your night and weekend staff. This requires creativity, but it's well worth the effort since it results in captured leads.

3. Train those in your hierarchy, or what I refer to as your back-up team.

4. Implement systems for measuring performance to ensure the system is working the way it should.

CREATING A SALES-CENTERED CULTURE

It's time to raise the bar, and it will not be easy. Most organizations in our industry do not demonstrate the most cohesive team environment. Typically, the executive director is heading up operations and has no idea what the sales department is doing; the activities director is only handling programming and interacting with residents; the chef is focused only on food preparation; and so on. And while everyone is *doing* their best to *be* their best, they are largely working on their own rather than as team members.

A sales-centered culture is one where everyone works together for the common good of the community or company. Each department head knows what's going on with the other, through effective communication; they help one another when needed, and freely support the needs of the other departments. If this is not the case at your community, you need to immediately get with your department heads, express your concerns, and see what you can do to create a more unified team environment.

The exercises on the next page are designed to help you think through this concept in terms of your own community, and will help you begin to formulate your back-up team.

WOULD YOU CONSIDER YOUR COMMUNITY TO HAVE A SALES-CENTERED CULTURE?   ☐ YES   ☐ NO
EXPLAIN YOUR ANSWER BELOW.

_____

_____

_____

EXERCISE:
_____

What one action step can you take today or tomorrow to facilitate a sales-centered culture?

_____

_____

_____

EXERCISE:
_____

Make a list of three to five people within your community who are personable and have the ability to follow directions. These might be people you have noticed who interact well with residents, love their jobs, seek recognition, and love to contribute to the overall success of the community. Think outside the box!

People on this list might include your business manager, director of nursing, chef, activities director, etc. Don't forget to include yourself. More than likely, you will be first on the list.

1. _____

2. _____

3. _____

4. _____

5. _____

You now have your potential back-up team. These are the people you are going to work with to create a well-oiled machine. Your back-up team will be responsible for handling inquiry calls, walk-ins, and personal visits. Don't panic, you will learn a system that will ensure their success and, in turn, yours as well. Of the five listed above, pick the top three people you would like to have handling inquiries. Simply circle the numbers next to their names.

WHAT'S NEXT?

The next step is to consider your weekly schedule and determine if the three team members chosen can cover all of the shifts or just one. If they only work Monday through Friday from 9-5, then the back-up team you've created won't be effective. You may have to utilize all five people on your list or even add more names to cover nights and weekends. Thought this would be easy, huh? This is probably one of the most mundane things you will do in this series, but the end result will be an influx of new leads, without one extra dollar going into marketing efforts! You will be better at maximizing what you have already worked so hard to generate.

Considering what I just said, what other candidates might you consider for nights and weekends as part of your back-up team hierarchy?

1. _____

2. _____

3. _____

4. _____

5. _____

LIST INDIVIDUALS WHO MIGHT SERVE AS BACK-UP TEAM MEMBERS ON NIGHTS AND WEEKENDS

Covering these shifts is much more challenging, but we cannot neglect the fact that many people who inquire will do so in the evenings and on the weekends. It's our job to accommodate them, not the other way around. Think hard, who else might be on this list? Is there a great nurse who could participate? What about the maintenance man or a housekeeper? Just bear with me and list three more names.

1. _____

2. _____

3. _____

As mentioned previously, so long as these individuals can read and follow directions, as well as be personable, they will succeed as effective members of your back-up team. Some of the people listed are incredibly talented, untapped resources, and you will be surprised by the assistance they can provide, once asked.

INCENTIVES

You may be wondering, "Okay, how is Lucy, our housekeeper, going to respond when asked to handle an inquiry call?" Well, what I have found is...very well. People like to be thought of as capable and will often step up to the plate when asked. You just have to give them the opportunity to shine. A great mentor of mine once said to me, "Traci, you're just like a lump of coal!" Shocked, I said, "What do you mean?" She responded, "Each year, you just get more and more polished and here you are now...a diamond!" I didn't know that a lump of coal eventually turns into a diamond, did you? How many lumps of coal do you have in your organization that would prefer to shine like a dazzling diamond?

Considering that many of these individuals don't make a lot of money, I suggest that you use the power of praise and recognition for a job well done, as many people prefer recognition over money.

Other ideas may be to have a set of gift cards on hand to stores like Target, Barnes & Noble, Starbucks, and more. When your back-up team performs for you and schedules an on-site visit or successfully handles an inquiry, give them one. Think of the nurse who is short on cash and who can now go pick up a toy for her child. That's motivation!

SO WHAT EXACTLY DOES A BACK-UP TEAM MEMBER DO?

Back-up team members are your sales support team, but more than that, they are critical to the overall profitability of the company.

Example:
10 inquiries /week
x 40%
4 leads x $36,000 = $108,000/ year lost

NOW THAT I HAVE YOUR ATTENTION, LET'S ONCE AGAIN DISCUSS WHAT YOUR BACK-UP TEAM MEMBERS WILL DO

They will be available to spend quality time with prospective residents and their family members via handling telephone or walk-in inquiries, personal visits, and if needed on rare occasions, follow-up. Most importantly, they should be available for inquiries. The back-up team demonstrates that the customer is a top priority. Remember...

You never get a second chance to
make a great first impression.

BACK-UP TEAM (Sample)

Please direct inquiries to the appropriate person. If the first person on the list is out, defer to the second, and so on.

TIME	MON	TUES	WED	THURS	FRI
7a-9a	Mary Kim	Mary Kim	Mary Kim	Mary Kim	Mary Kim
9a-5p	Janet Greg Martha Ann Beth	Janet Greg Martha Ann Beth	Janet Greg Martha Ann Beth	Janet Greg Martha Ann Beth	Janet Greg Martha Ann
5p-12a	Kirt Sue Deb	Kirt Sue Deb	Kirt Sue Deb	Kirt Sue Deb	Kirt Sue Deb

WEEKENDS (Sample)

TIME	SAT	SUN
7a-9a	Janet	Janet
9a-5p	Sandy Ron Shelly	Sandy Ron Shelly
5p-12a	Jack Ella	Jack Ella

*Individuals on the back-up team should alert you when they are going to be unavailable.

BACK-UP TEAM HIERARCHY

Please direct the call to the appropriate person.
If the first person on the list is out, defer to the second, and so on.

TIME	MON		TUES	WED	THURS	FRI
7a-9a	1. 2.					
9a-5p	1. 2. 3. 4. 5.					
5p-12a	1. 2. 3.					

TIME	SAT	SUN
7a-9a	1.	
9a-5p	1. 2. 3.	
5p-12a	1. 2.	

TRAINING

Now that you understand what a hierarchy is—the order in which the members of your back-up team take inquiries—let's discuss what they should do when their number is up and it's their turn to work with the prospect.

The entire next segment provides the actual "How to," but before going into the nuts and bolts of the selling system, I want to caution you. It's critical that you take the time to *train all members* of your back-up team and that you follow up and do refresher training regularly. If not, the system you spend time on developing will not stick. Eliminating mismanaged calls takes regular maintenance. However, with a little effort every day, you can eliminate them forever and recapture millions in lost revenues company-wide.

On average, you can easily train back-up team members in just one hour. The key to real success is role-playing, follow-up coaching, and accountability.

RECEPTIONIST

The other thing you must do is ensure there is an effective communication system set up with your receptionist. A system is no good if it does not work. I've talked with many people who have told me, "We have a hierarchy and we do train our team." But when we shop them, we find out their system isn't working. The typical problem: the person answering the phones has no idea there is a system at all, and therefore can't do his or her job of getting the inquirer to the right person at the right time. Talk about missed opportunity! You must have some type of call log where the people on the hierarchy can log in and out, a dry erase board where they can check in and out, or a daily schedule that is posted the evening prior so the morning receptionist knows exactly what's going on.

Communicating with the front desk is critical to your overall success. If you completed the hierarchy form on the prior pages, this is a great starting place.

DON'T BE FOOLED

Again, this process seems easy but, as you have noticed, there are lots of details and follow-through is critical to making the system work. On the following page is a checklist. If you are an executive director, I challenge you to address inquiries in your weekly meeting. Take just two minutes and acknowledge the people who completed inquiry sheets, address mismanaged calls that were perhaps identified via a mystery shop, and keep the training up-to-date.

Mismanaged Call Success Checklist

1 Develop a strategy to create more of a sales-centered culture.
Projected completion date:

2 Determine how much money mismanaged calls are costing you annually so you can communicate this to your team and create urgency.
Projected completion date:

3 Develop a five-level hierarchy and formalize it.
Projected completion date:

4 Determine what your incentives will be for the participating back-up team members who are not part of the actual sales team.
Projected completion date:

5 Set a training date for the receptionist.
Projected completion date:

6 Set a training date for the back-up team.
Projected completion date:

7 Schedule a series of mystery shops to test your system (visit www.bildandco.com or call 1.800.640.0688 to learn how we can help).
Projected completion date:

List other tasks you would like to complete as part of this effort:

- _____
- _____
- _____

CHAPTER THREE

THE INQUIRY SYSTEM

FIRST CONTACT

"Get them in the door and my people can close them!" It's a phrase I've heard many times. My standard response? Exactly! It's much easier to close a prospect once on site; it's getting them in the door that's the difficult part.

Today, people have options. In the past, there was one, maybe two communities that people would inquire about. Now there is a community every mile or so, it seems. What should cause concern is the level of service people receive when calling senior housing communities. Mystery shop study after study, including our own, reveal that when people call seeking Independent and Assisted Living, Skilled Nursing, and Rehab, the "service" they receive is nothing short of frightening. Sales counselors consistently spew information and fail to listen to what's important to those inquiring about their products. Talk about missed opportunities!

Here's what too often happens when people call in and get through to someone in sales (or a member of the back-up team) who (supposedly) can help them. Instead of finding their needs and building value, people are selling benefits and listing features that they find appealing about their communities. The result is a frustrated caller who is further turned off by your product. The media has already created a negative image of the senior housing industry. People seem convinced that everything is a nursing home and that every nursing home is bad. We have to dispel that myth, *starting with first contact.* However, what do you think is going to happen when a prospective client calls and hears this:

"We have 24-hour nursing, three meals a day with restaurant style dining, a snack available in the evening, housekeeping services, and we change the sheets twice a week. Let's see... we have transportation, all kinds of activities from bingo to book clubs, we have weekly trips to the grocery and to various stores such as Walmart, the mall, and once a month we go to restaurants, whether it's Mexican, Italian, pizza, whatever our residents feel like doing. There is just so much to do here!" (And on and on.)

At this point, some prospects may immediately begin to second guess their decision. In turn, many choose other options: a smaller home or condo, moving in with a family member, staying put, or hiring home health. These other options are really your biggest competitors. This type of selling validates what they think they already know about your services and, in essence, confirms their fears that what they are doing will not be a positive experience.

THE GOOD NEWS

We *can* change public perception by providing world class customer service. I must warn you, however, that good intentions to provide great service rarely produce consistent results. In fact, good intentions alone produce absolutely nothing.

YOU MUST HAVE SYSTEMS IN PLACE TO ENSURE SERVICE IS WORLD CLASS AND CONSISTENT OVER TIME

This section will help you to implement a structured sales system for incoming calls or walk-ins who are inquiring about your community. Because it's a system, it can be implemented at all of your communities, whether there are four, forty, or four hundred. The most difficult part of this process? Changing human behavior! The system is easy; changing habits is not. You have to keep your eye on the end goals: a fully occupied building that is maximizing its revenue potential; a sales team that is working smart, not hard—working less, yet producing more; and families who feel excited about their loved one's move.

WHAT IS HAPPENING TODAY

In the last chapter I advised you to mystery shop your community for the sole purpose of identifying what is happening to your leads. Are they being captured or mismanaged? I now challenge you to mystery shop your community with a sole focus on the sales counselor. Where performance is measured, it can be improved. Without evidence of what is happening today, it will be hard to create buy-in tomorrow to implement training systems. Make sure that your mystery shops are recorded. People must be able to hear the evidence so there is no "he said, she said."

If you would like for us to do this for you, simply call our office at 800.640.0688 or visit our website at www.BildandCo. com. We record our shops and also provide a written evaluation that identifies specific information relating to likability and sales-ability. There are many companies that provide this service. What's important is that you hire somebody to do it.

SET A COMPLETION DATE WHEN YOU WILL HAVE MYSTERY SHOPS ORDERED ON YOUR SALES COUNSELOR(S):

SET A COMPLETION DATE WHEN YOU WILL HAVE THE MYSTERY SHOP RESULTS IN YOUR HANDS TO REVIEW:

Once you see the value in these, you will want to take advantage of the opportunity to have shops done on a regular basis. The results are invaluable.

SHOP RESULTS

Odds are, your shop results will reveal the following:

- ❑ One to two questions from the sales counselor, no more. Typically, the question will be something like, "What made you decide to call us today?" If more questions are asked, they are typically yes or no questions, such as, "Is your mom ambulatory? Does she need help with grooming? Does she need assistance with medication?" The problem with such questions is, they yield very little information and fail to move the sales process forward.

- ❑ Once the sales counselor feels he or she has enough information to sell, you will begin to hear a rote listing of services, similar to our "laundry list" phone call from last chapter: "...24-hour nursing staff, restaurant style dining...housekeeping services...laundry once a week, transportation, a library...bingo and bridge, movies..." and on and on and on. Literally, many people will talk and talk until they run out of breath.

Sound familiar? Studies have shown that the reason people do this is the fear of being at a loss for words. The last thing in the world that salespeople want is to appear like they don't have knowledge of their product or service, thus the chatter. People don't mean to do this, it just happens; it's simply habit.

- ❑ Once the sales counselors provided the listing of services, they typically offered to send a packet of information. "Would you like for me to send you a brochure?" They then proceeded to get the address and, many times, neglected to get a phone number. How can follow-up take place without a number? And e-mail? Forget it. No one is asking for this, and it's a shame because seniors are the fastest growing demographic using the web. Additionally, it's their children who are often inquiring. Think about it, do you personally know anyone who does not have and use e-mail? Why are we not using this free means of communication?

❏ The close: rarely will a sales counselor ask a caller to come in for a personal visit. The brochure seems to be the typical close. The assumption is that the person calling will get the brochure and be so excited that she will call back to book a tour. This is a costly assumption. On the rare occasion when sales counselors do ask for an appointment, it's normally very passive, "Would you like to stop by and take a look at our community sometime?" That doesn't really motivate the person on the other end of the line. He or she is probably thinking, *I don't know, should I?* If *we're* not passionate and convinced that this is the best decision they can make, why should *they* be excited about it? Again, all we're really doing is encouraging them to investigate other options.

THE RESULT?

You may not want to hear this, because it hurts. Hundreds of thousands of dollars of potential revenue is being left on the table for your competitors to freely take. Competitors include other communities, home health care, condos, family care, and more. Our industry is much too laid back; there is no urgency, little strategy, and a fear of selling in general. But if you follow the system I'm about to introduce, you will never feel like you are selling again. Your goal is to help people identify their needs and in turn, build value in regard to your services. It's a win-win for everyone involved. The reality is that the very person who hates feeling like a "salesperson" is coming across as such, and doesn't even realize it. Play the recordings of your mystery shops for your sales team and watch them cringe. This will also provide the motivation needed to put systems in place to ensure it doesn't happen again.

A SPECIAL NOTE IF YOU WORK WITHIN A CCRC ENVIRONMENT

Okay, you are either going to love me or hate me, because I am going to be blunt. I work with a lot of CCRC communities, and each time the relationship begins, I am told the following: "Traci, our sales counselors are different." Upon further discussion, I am typically told that the CCRC sales counselors are more savvy than your typical marketers, that they have excellent selling skills but are just missing "something," that they don't need to use all of our systems, "just a select few," and that they are the cream of the crop.

I love the fact that CCRC managers are so passionate about their people. Yet my job is to be unbiased and to provide the facts, whether it's something one wants to hear or not. The biggest difference I have seen with CCRC sales counselors, as compared to others in our industry, is that they are deeply committed to their communities and have extensive experience with the CCRC model. Most have been with their respective communities for a decade or more and that indeed is impressive. Because of their experience, they are very knowledgeable about their product and have the facts down, solid. I am certain that a CCRC sales counselor who takes a test would pass it with flying colors.

However, should they be mystery shopped by my company, and tested on their sales and relationship building skills, most would perform at a level they or their superiors would consider shocking. Sadly, it would be a far cry from passing with flying colors. Case in point: I just conducted a seminar for an amazing Life Care Community in Florida. While training on this very point, I offered to call three of their biggest competitors. Due to my experience with CCRC and Life Care communities, I had no doubt what I would find and I knew the experience would solidify the training I was providing to this great team. I put my cell on speakerphone and began making my calls.

Three for three, each community failed miserably. Not one asked me more than a single question, each pre-qualified me up front, with no regard to my needs, explained pricing, entry fees, refunds and more (without my prompting), and all actively pushed their brochures. Unfortunately, this was not an anomaly—but the norm. If you are with a CCRC or Life Care Community, do not kid yourself. You, like your Independent and Assisted Living peers, need the systems outlined in this book. Your model, more than all others, has been the most negatively impacted by the Great Recession.

Because people need to sell their homes to fund the entry fees, the sales environment is much more challenging. The tactics you have used for the past decade are not nearly as effective as the systems outlined in this book. For my CCRC and Life Care readers, here are a few specific points I want to make so that you can better understand how this book applies to you.

❑ Selling a CCRC or Life Care community is the same as selling Independent Living, Assisted Living, Memory Care, or Skilled Nursing. Yes, you have a more complex product to sell and a longer sales cycle, but your buyer, just like the buyers of the other products mentioned, will buy when the value of moving exceeds the pain of what they have to experience to become a resident at your community. For you, it may be the pain of discounting their homes another 15% to facilitate sales. For the Assisted Living prospect, it's the pain associated with one's guilt over not caring for a loved one personally. This emotional pain can actually be more challenging than that of simply getting less money for a home—my point being that, no matter what you are selling, you must know how to find needs and build strong value.

❑ CCRC and Life Care prospects are calling because of a need. Most sales counselors I work with say that I don't understand and that their prospects don't have needs because they are independent. Yes, this may be the case for a handful of your prospects, but I know, from my personal experience in working with many CCRC communities to close sales, that the majority *are* need-driven; they simply are not telling you that up front. With our average prospect being in their early to mid-eighties, there are needs that have driven them to your community. One of my wonderful clients, Wendy Horn, calls this a "life scare." She says that at some point, there has been a scare in your prospect's life that has led him or her to you. It might be a personal health scare of some sort, or that of a friend. Yet when these prospects call, they are not going to tell you that; they will simply say they saw your ad or were referred by a friend. It's your job as a sales professional to dig down and get to the core of what really drove them to your community, and that takes skill.

❏ I understand that entry fee communities are limited to a select few who have the financial qualifications to make a move to such a community. The most troubling thing I find when shopping and training sales counselors selling CCRC and Life Care products, is that they consistently attempt to pre-qualify within the first two minutes of the phone call. Instead of finding needs and building value, they are dropping entry fee numbers, monthly rates, the percentage that is refundable and, in short, confusing the heck out of their callers.

It's a classic case of putting the cart before the horse. I realize that some callers are well educated in what a CCRC and/or Life Care community is, but even they want to know that someone is sincerely interested in them, not just their financial outlook. Even I, having extensive experience with such products, become confused when shopping entry fee communities. A quick attempt by a sales counselor to pre-qualify a prospect, so as not to waste their time, ends up instead costing them what might have been their next resident. It is critical that you don't attempt to pre-qualify up front and offer to send a brochure, but that you instead immerse yourself in this chapter and trust that the systems outlined will work for you, because they will.

When using the inquiry system I am about to teach, know that if indeed a "red flag" comes up during your conversation, you can then go there and dig into finances to ensure you don't waste your time. Possible red flags might be the mention of Medicaid, certain healthcare needs, and so on. You will know them when you hear them. If you don't, just hold off on the financial part and remember that your sole goal of the inquiry call is to get people in the door. I promise, you will see the red flags when they are there and weed out those who are not qualified. You will also end up with many leads you would have otherwise disqualified and that actually have the means to move to your community but were not wearing their entire stories on their sleeves.

❏ Typically, I find that the CCRC and Life Care sales counselors seek to first send a brochure. The number one most important skill factor required to drive occupancy is to *get more people in the door*. Would you rather a hot prospect meet you or your brochure? Which will make a better impression? I think it's safe to say, it's you! Stop offering brochures and, instead, start asking for an appointment. It is crucial that you schedule a meeting while your prospect is in the shopping mode, and waiting for a brochure to arrive in the course of a week can be detrimental.

❏ Lastly, I find that many CCRC and Life Care sales counselors rely on their properties to sell themselves. It is important to remember that people are not buying the building but, instead, the experience. Although it's tempting to just "let the building show itself," it's your ability to drill down and get to the core of the prospect's needs that will close the deal. The wonderful building is the by-product.

Some of my greatest clients run entry fee communities. I always say that when I grow old I am going to move to a Life Care community; it just makes sense. What you are offering is incredible, yet *how* it's offered must change.

MY FIRST ENTRY FEE PROJECT

ACTS Retirement Life Communities was my first such client in the senior housing industry. I can still remember to this day how intimidated I was. The average tenure of their Life Care consultants was seventeen years and their company occupancy was 92%. I remember thinking, "Boy, how am I going to grow occupancy by a good 5% with a team so experienced and set in their ways?" Well, the answer was, I trusted my systems. I coached their sales organization for six months and by the end of our training, they had grown company-wide occupancy from 92% to 99.4%, across seventeen properties, a company record. I heard from many Life Care consultants, "Wow, Traci, you can actually teach old dogs new tricks" and, "I'm connecting with people like never before and can remember why I fell in love with this job in the first place."

I'm not going to say it was easy, and implementing the training really wasn't the hard part; it was changing people's habits—that was the true challenge. The best part was that the team respected the fact that Louise Franklin, their leader, found the value in hiring me and in turn chose to give it a try. Instead of sulking and continuing to do things their own way to prove I had nothing to bring to the table, they gave the training a shot. With each success, their confidence grew and they tried more. Together, we made amazing things happen at ACTS Retirement Life, and I am forever grateful to Louise and her team. That experience shaped me as a person and helped me to better understand what it takes to transform the skills and habits of people with great talent and tenure.

YOUR OPPORTUNITY

If you run or sell for an entry fee project, the systems I am about to present can have more impact than any other set of tools you've utilized since starting your job. What might seem basic to you (like asking questions and listening), is probably an opportunity that can have more impact on your results than you could ever imagine. Because your prospects have fewer needs than our Independent, Assisted Living, Memory Care, and SNF readers, it is more important than ever to implement what I'm about to teach you. Give it a try and you'll see for yourself what I'm talking about.

LET'S GET STARTED

We discussed the importance of having a system in place to eliminate mismanaged calls. Doing this will immediately impact revenue in a positive way and provide a stronger return on marketing efforts. Now we need to focus on the system needed to ensure that, once calls get through, they reach someone who can help, that needs are identified, value built, and a personal visit scheduled. This is our only objective, nothing else.

Many times, sales counselors get ahead of themselves and, instead of focusing on the caller and getting an appointment scheduled, they are thinking about the deposit or move-in potential. Everything happens one step at a time. The first step is to just get a visit, whether it's at your community, the caller's home, or the hospital. I have found that this creates incredible relief for sales counselors. They like the idea of focusing on nothing but getting a visit scheduled. Suddenly, the call doesn't seem so overwhelming.

WHAT'S THE KEY TO GETTING THE PERSONAL VISIT SCHEDULED?

You must identify needs and build value. The value felt must exceed the pain or hassle of coming in. You must get people over the value threshold. The value built must exceed the pain of getting in their cars and driving to your community, addressing their fears, guilt, and taking time from their schedules to come see you. If you can't do this, they will not come. What the caller is really asking is, "What's in it for me?" It doesn't matter how nice you are, how compassionate or friendly. The inquirer may like you, but not see the value in coming in. Do you see the difference? We must get people within our industry focused on finding needs and building value—not just selling.

THE FIRST STEP

Upon receiving a transferred call, the sales counselor or member of the back-up team, whoever is taking the call, must first get permission to ask questions of the caller or visitor. Doing this transfers control of the call from the inquirer to the sales counselor.

This is critical to getting results. Here is how the call might go:

Hi, Mrs. Smith, this is Traci, how can I help you today?

Yes, I just wanted to get some information on your community. How much is it to live there?

I would be more than happy to give you that information, Mrs. Smith. Do you mind if I ask you a few quick questions so I know what kind of pricing to give you?

Sure...

Mission accomplished! Doing this immediately transfers control and in turn will allow the sales counselor to focus the caller on her needs versus the price. It's important not to assume that people really only want prices or brochures. Many times they just don't know what else to say. Odds are, your caller is in unfamiliar territory, and is uncomfortable and defensive as a result.

As you will see, the system I'm about to teach you is not scripted. I don't believe in scripts. It is, however, a system, and the system must be followed for it to be effective. Therefore, in your own words, whenever someone walks in or calls, you want to get permission to ask questions as soon as you can. If the first thing the caller says is, "Can I ask a few questions about your facility?" answer their questions briefly and then obtain permission to ask your own. You want to take control so you can better serve the caller in the end.

After getting a *yes* response, you will then go into the needs identification stage, which is certainly the most important part of the sales process. I want to point out that in studies done by my company, we have found that if you don't first gain permission to ask questions prior to asking them, then people get antsy and uncomfortable. In listening to sales calls, my personal opinion is that prospects don't know what's going on or how many questions you are going to ask. They feel out of control. Simply by obtaining permission to ask questions, you eliminate this obstacle altogether.

MAY I ASK YOU A FEW QUICK QUESTIONS SO I KNOW BEST HOW TO HELP YOU?

NEEDS IDENTIFICATION
Your objectives in this phase are to:

- ❏ uncover needs to create value
- ❏ relate and empathize with prospects
- ❏ listen

Asking questions to uncover needs makes it clear that you care about what people feel and think. People really appreciate this, and can tell when you're sincerely interested. **Remember, people buy when they feel their needs are going to be met.** To help you accomplish this objective, we have created and tested a solid series of questions that are designed to uncover the prospect's needs and build value in regard to your community.

It's been proven that the ability of sales counselors to ask a series of questions in a specific sequence is a key component to driving occupancy. I have been teaching this exact philosophy to people just like you for over two decades. Now we have proof to back it up. The best news is, you don't have to formulate these questions yourself—we've done the hard part for you. We have tested these questions and continue to research their impact on prospective residents to make sure you have the most current, effective tools in hand. Our questions are outlined in a standardized form, called Connection Sheets™.

WHAT IS A CONNECTION SHEET?

It's a tool designed to identify needs and build value in regard to the product or services you are offering. This tool consists of a series of open-ended questions that allow prospects to focus on what's important to them—not to you—in a community they might choose. We called it a "Connection Sheet" because there is nothing more important in a people business such as yours than connecting.

WHY CONNECTION SHEETS ARE CRITICAL TO MAXIMIZING OCCUPANCY

In an industry-wide study referenced previously and done by Promatura, 494 random telephone mystery shops were conducted. As a whole, the industry received an "F" grade. This study provided the evidence needed to shed light on the severity of the problem facing sales professionals in our industry. I will continue to give you information on this study and others as we move forward. Things must change! Here are some of the common mistakes I see on a regular basis.

COMMON MISTAKES THAT SALES COUNSELORS MAKE:

- ❏ They fail to take the time needed to ask questions and learn what's important to the prospect. In essence, they talk more than they listen.

- ❏ They randomly list services, with no consideration as to what the prospect needs; it's a one-size-fits-all approach. Many in our industry refer to this as "verbal vomiting!"

- ❏ They lack empathy.

- ❏ They make assumptions as to who can afford their community and who cannot.

- ❏ They fail to collect valuable contact information.

- ❏ They oftentimes give the prospect the impression that they have been interrupted and taken away from something more important.

❏ They freely offer to send informational packets and give prices out over the phone.

Need I say more? The exciting thing is that all of these mistakes can be fixed with a good dose of training. As Oprah Winfrey says, "You can't do better until you know better." I believe that people selling senior housing services have their prospects' best interests at heart. The troubling thing is that it doesn't always come across this way. My goal is to help you match your desire to help people with their desire to find a solution to their problems.

TAKE A LOOK AT THE CONNECTION SHEETS ON THE FOLLOWING TWO PAGES, THEN COMPLETE THE EXERCISE.

WALK-IN	**Inquiry Connection**
PHONE	**Sheet ADULT CHILD**

| WEB LEAD | TEAM MEMBER | DATE | TIME |

NOTES

I would be more than happy to get you the information you're looking for. Before doing so, do you mind if I ask you a few quick questions so I know best how to help you?

Can I get your name _____ Phone: _____

Family member's name: _____

What made you decide to call us today? _____

What's your greatest concern at this time? _____

How is this impacting you? _____

Where does your _____ currently live? _____

Is he / she aware that you're looking? _____ How does he or she feel about the move? _____

Is anyone else going to be supporting you in making this decision? _____

What's most important to you regarding the community you choose? _____

Tell me about your _____ 's daily routine. _____

What does he/she enjoy doing? _____

If we could do one thing to improve your loved one's quality of life, what would it be? _____

So based on what you've told me it sounds like... (recap conversation) _____

The next step is _____

Offer options of two _____

May I ask how you heard about us? _____

Contact information: Phone _____ E-mail _____

Mailing address _____

CS 2.0-1-2015   TRAINING   COACHING   MYSTERY SHOPPING   MARKETING   SOCIAL MEDIA   CRM   BILD   BILD&CO

THE INQUIRY SYSTEM

Inquiry Connection Sheet
PROSPECTIVE RESIDENT

TEAM MEMBER	DATE	TIME

I would be more than happy to get you the information you're looking for. Before doing so, do you mind if I ask you a few quick questions so I know best how to help you?

Can I get your name_____ Phone: _____

What made you decide to call us today? _____

What's most important to you regarding the community you choose? _____

At this point, what other options are you considering? _____

Tell me about your daily routine. How do you like to spend your time? _____

What do you enjoy most about your current lifestyle? What are you looking to gain? _____

Is anyone else going to be supporting you in making this decision? _____

So based on what you've told me it sounds like .. (recap conversation)

The next step is ..

Offer options of two

May I ask how you heard about us? _____

Contact information
Phone_____ E-mail _____

Mailing address_____

CS 2.0 ± 2015   TRAINING   COACHING   MYSTERY SHOPPING   MARKETING   SOCIAL MEDIA   CRM   BILD   BILD & CO
INTEGRATED MULTI-FAMILY SOLUTIONS
800 646.1638
bildandco.com

These are two of our most popular Connection Sheets. We have discovered that simply telling a sales counselor to remember to ask lots of great open-ended questions is just not enough. Our studies have found that people must be given the questions in advance.

WHY?

If we do not provide you with the Connection Sheets, odds are you will remember to ask one, maybe two questions before you go into selling mode. Even then, the questions may not be open-ended, but yes or no questions. If you doubt this, record yourself making calls without the Connection Sheet in front of you. You will find my observation to be very true.

The fact is, in sales, it's a stressful environment. People are nervous and can't think quickly enough on their feet to remember to ask as many as eight to ten great, open-ended questions. Likewise, why should you have to memorize or remember all these questions? It's much easier to just pull out a Connection Sheet and get to the needs of the individual you are speaking with.

EXERCISE:

Record the next inquiry you receive—your side of the conversation only—*not using* the Inquiry Connection Sheet. Once done, answer the following questions:

How many open-ended questions did you ask? _____

How many YES or NO questions did you ask? _____

How many physical/medical needs did you identify? _____

How many emotional needs did you identify? _____

Next, put an Inquiry Connection Sheet on your desk and when the next inquiry call comes in, use it in full. Be sure to ask as many of the questions as you can; don't stop at just two or three because the meatiest questions are toward the end. Using this tool, record your call and, again, listen to it once you are done.

How many open-ended questions did you ask? _____

How many YES or NO questions did you ask? _____

How many physical/medical needs did you identify? _____

How many emotional needs did you identify? _____

Would you say that you were able to identify more needs using the Connection Sheet?

_____

How far into the Connection Sheet did you go (How many questions)? _____

What difference most stood out to you?

_____

_____

_____

Common Mistakes

1   **Not using the FULL Inquiry Connection Sheet**

If you did not identify enough needs to experience the difference between using the Inquiry Connection Sheet and not using it, odds are you didn't follow through on it in its entirety. When first using this tool, many people ask just two to three questions and assume they already know the rest of the answers. This is a tragic mistake because the fact is, there is no way you can know what their thoughts are emotionally without their telling you firsthand. If you don't ask, you won't know—you will only be assuming and placing them in a box with everyone else. In sales, it's emotion that drives people to take action, and it's up to you to tap into that emotion.

2   **Attempting to book a tour too soon**

The other thing people do is to get ahead of themselves. As a result of learning so much, so fast, many people find it difficult to hold back and continue to ask the remaining questions from the Connection Sheet. Instead of exercising patience and asking all of the questions, they stop and ask for the appointment. If you do this, realize that you may ask too soon and that you have not yet built enough value to get them to step out of their comfort zones and come in. My suggestion is to play it safe, with what's proven to work, so that you can get the result you seek. *Use the full Inquiry Connection Sheet!*

VISUALIZE A TREE

If you will, take a moment to visualize a tree. Think of the Connection Sheet as the trunk. All the questions on the Connection Sheet are representative of the trunk. Have you ever seen a tree without branches? Neither have I. When you are in the process of asking the pre-planned questions from the Connection Sheet, feel free to branch off. What I mean by this is, ask more questions that are not on the sheet, yet are directly related to one you might have just asked. Consider the example below.

EXAMPLE:

Jack, what was it that made you decide to call in to learn more about us today?

Well, I saw your ad and was curious...

At this point, you are probably thinking it would not seem appropriate to go to the next question of, "Are you looking for a family member?" Instead, you are wondering, what is it about the ad that drove him to pick up the phone? What is the driving reason? If this is what you are thinking, then by all means, branch off and ask.

Is something going on in particular with yourself or a loved one that made our ad stand out to you?

Well yes, my dad has been falling a lot lately and I'm worried to death about him being at home alone.

I'm so sorry to hear that. (Time to branch again) **Is there anything you can attribute the falling to in particular?**

Really, it just started happening after his last stroke. He has had two minor strokes and the only effects we have seen are the tripping and the three falls he has had, which are terrifying.

(Again, branch!) **Have there been any additional health problems that have resulted from the actual falls themselves?**

Nothing more than some bruising and a twisted knee. But at his age, every fall is a huge risk.

How old is your dad?

86.

Now onto the next question...

Does he know you are looking into assisted living?

Yes.

How does he feel about it?

He is not happy about it, but realizes that he has to get out of his home and into a safe environment.

May I ask, what's most important to you in regard to a community you might choose for your dad?

That he is happy.

(Branch!) **May I ask, what makes him happy?**

Do you get the hang of it? This is a system, not a script. You follow the system to drive the result, yet adapt it to the current situation. The more you learn, the better and more success you will have. The trunk is the Connection Sheet, the branches are the additional questions that grow off of the trunk, and then we have leaves. Yes, leaves! If you will, visualize the most beautiful tree you have ever seen. A big tree, with yellow, orange, and red leaves...think of this as a visual. As you branch off, make sure that you add leaves, which correlate to stories, examples, and services that fit with what your inquirer is saying is important to him or her. We want prospects to visualize life at your community and feel validated that they called the right place. The entire next segment, on needs matching, is about the leaves.

EXCEPTIONS

#1 THEY WON'T ANSWER YOUR QUESTIONS

There will be times when it will not be appropriate to use the full Inquiry Connection Sheet. For example, if you say to your prospects, "Do you mind if I ask you a few quick questions?" and they say, "No," well, what are you going to do? This is very rare and I personally have seen it happen maybe five times in all the years I've been teaching this system. If it does happen, then just ask how you may help them and once you've answered their questions, give it another shot by saying, "Now do you mind if I take just a moment to learn a little bit more about you?" You will be surprised to find that the answer will more than likely be a yes.

#2 THEY WANT TO BOOK AN IMMEDIATE APPOINTMENT

If someone calls in and immediately says, "I would like to come visit your community," go ahead and book the appointment time and date. Once that has been established, say, "So I can better prepare for your visit, do you mind if I ask you a few quick questions?" Again, they will likely respond with a yes, which gives you permission to utilize the Connection Sheet. If for any reason the caller does not have time to talk further, simply make it a point to complete the Connection Sheet first thing upon their showing up for the tour.

You must find needs if you expect to build value, and doing so will dramatically shorten your sales cycle and make for a better experience for both you and the inquirer. Keep in mind that the main reason you want to complete the Connection Sheet prior to the visit is so that you can be proactive and plan a visit built around their needs. Doing so will make a tremendous impact on your prospects and, in turn, get them to make a deposit and move in sooner.

INQUIRY CONNECTION SHEET STUDY

Are you wondering just how important it really is to use the Inquiry Connection Sheets? Here are some interesting statistics we have compiled.

- ❏ When a full Connection Sheet is used, the average mystery shop score is 92%.

- ❏ When a partial Connection Sheet is used, consisting of three to four questions only, the score drops to 72%.

- ❏ When no Connection Sheet is used, the score is a sad 32%.

The mystery shop is a reflection of service. This is powerful information and something I hope you will take seriously.

Success means doing what you have to do, when you have to do it, whether you feel like doing it or not. No one really wants to use the Connection Sheet; it's much easier to just wing it. However, if you want a full building, getting more people in the door is key to making that happen. You must be prepared. That's really what success is about: preparation meeting opportunity. It's not about luck!

NEEDS MATCH

Your objectives in this phase are to:

- ❏ share stories, services, and examples that the prospect can relate to as you uncover their needs

- ❏ convey compassion and empathy

Again referencing Dr. Margaret Wylde's and David Smith's study, they outlined specific factors associated with successful sales discussions. I felt it appropriate to bring this to your attention as we begin to discuss the importance of needs matching.

STUDY

In their study, it was determined that few of the sales counselors demonstrated the ability to learn about the customer and then apply this information to show how their community will solve difficulties the customer and the family are experiencing, and how their community will best meet the needs of the prospective resident. There were several attributes of the discussions with the sales personnel that contributed to successful sales efforts. These were related to the ability of the sales counselor to:

1. Understand the emotional and lifestyle impact of the move on the resident and family, and RELATE the benefits of the community to them.

2. Probe the abilities of the prospective resident to socialize and get around the community, and to clarify the benefits of the services of the community as they are specifically related to the prospect.

3. Relate the value of the community to both the prospective resident and the family, discuss how the community is a good solution for the prospect, and differentiate the community from others.

4. Establish a sense of trust and a positive mood.

5. Advance the sale and be available to the customer.

6. Engage in the practice of selling the community.

7. Counsel the resident and family about moving.

The factors used in this study were identified through factor analysis. Factor analysis is a statistical method that enables researchers to reduce a large number of variables to a smaller number of variables, or factors. In this study, the factors were a cluster of variables that were highly inter-correlated with the shoppers' rating of the communities they were very likely to choose as a place for their parents, based on their discussions with the seller. These seven factors accounted for 88% of the variability in the ratings of shoppers.

NEEDS MATCH!

As a coach, one of the most difficult challenges I, as well as my coaching team, have is teaching our students the importance of matching specific stories, examples, and services to the individual needs of the prospect they are speaking to. Doing so validates the caller and makes one feel good about the decision to pick up the phone and contact you. Remember, this is where you fill the tree with beautiful leaves! See the example below.

NEEDS MATCH EXAMPLE:

In using the Adult Child Inquiry Connection Sheet, you ask the question, "What is most important to you in regard to the community you might choose for your mom?"

The caller responds with, "I want her to get the help she needs, while maintaining her independence and sense of freedom. In no way do I want her to feel as though she has been stuck somewhere. I want her to enjoy her move, to love her environment, and feel like she belongs."

Being that the caller just shared what is most important, this would be an ideal place to needs match. Here is an example of how you would make a match:

> *I can completely understand what you're saying. We had a new resident move in recently and her main concern was losing her freedom; we assured her that it would not happen and that, in fact, she would have more freedom due to not being confined to her home since she*

no longer drives. Rose has only been living here for two months and I have to tell you that she has become a resident favorite among both the staff and people who live here, due to her involvement in everything from yoga to movie night. If there is something going on, Rose is the first one there. She actually told us that she didn't realize how much she was missing by being stuck at home alone. Basically, Rose does what she wants, when she wants, yet still has the security of our staff, should something happen that's unexpected. She really has the best of both worlds, and that is what we would like to do for your mom.

When needs matching, you can be brief or a bit extensive. There is no right or wrong way to do this. What matters is that you don't start "selling" your community. You simply want to share a story or item of interest that prospects can relate to and that will put their minds at ease.

EXERCISE:

How might you needs match upon hearing the same answer as described above by our prospect Mary? What could you share as a result of your experiences?

_____

_____

_____

RULE OF THUMB

As you use the Connection Sheets, you do not have to needs match after every single question. You want to be continually looking for great opportunities to tie something in that is relevant and powerful.

When you hear something that is really important—a concern or something that is what I call a hot button—this is when you should needs match. Doing so demonstrates that you are listening, that you care, understand, and can relate. It makes people feel at ease and as though they are not alone in what they are going through. More importantly, we have found that people crave empathy and needs matching allows that compassion and empathy to come across to the prospect.

EXERCISE:

Use the Connection Sheet on the following page in a role-play setting. As you do the role-play, be sure to needs match as you complete the Connection Sheet.

THE INQUIRY SYSTEM

Inquiry Connection
Sheet ADULT CHILD

| TEAM MEMBER | DATE | TIME |

I would be more than happy to get you the information you're looking for. Before doing so, do you mind if I ask you a few quick questions so I know best how to help you?

Can I get your name _____ Phone: _____

Family member's name: _____

What made you decide to call us today? _____

_____

What's your greatest concern at this time? _____

How is this impacting you?

Where does your _____ currently live? _____

Is he / she aware that you're looking? _____ How does he or she feel about the move?

_____

Is anyone else going to be supporting you in making this decision? _____

What's most important to you regarding the community you choose? _____

_____

Tell me about your _____ 's daily routine. _____

_____

What does he/she enjoy doing? _____

_____

If we could do one thing to improve your loved one's quality of life, what would it be? _____

So based on what you've told me it sounds like... (recap conversation) _____

The next step is _____

Offer options of two _____

May I ask how you heard about us? _____

Contact information: Phone _____ E-mail _____

Mailing address _____

TRAINING   COACHING   MYSTERY SHOPPING   MARKETING   SOCIAL MEDIA   CRM   **BILD**   BILD&CO
INTEGRATED HEALTHCARE SOLUTIONS
800.640.0688
bildandco.com

THE CLOSE

Your objectives in this phase are to:

- ❏ repeat needs back

- ❏ utilize the optional close

Human nature tells us that people take action based on their needs or motivations. This is the key to the close, showing that there is something in it for the prospect, not just a sale for you. Many times, inquirers don't know what it is they want until you begin to ask questions. For this reason, it's critical that when closing, you repeat the needs back to build value and validate their reason for calling. This is the *Jerry McGuire*, "You had me at hello" moment!

After repeating the needs back, go right into a confident optional close. This means that you should give callers a choice of two things they can pick from, and that you want them to pick from...meaning "no" is not one of the options. The most common close is, "So do you think you would like to come by sometime for a tour?" This makes me wonder, *I don't know, should I?* How can they be confident in their decision if you're not? Instead, you want to offer them a choice of today or tomorrow, morning or afternoon, not the choice of yes or no.

EXAMPLE:

> *Mrs. Smith, based on what you've told me, it sounds like you have been caring for your husband for over five years. You are exhausted, both physically and mentally. Is that correct?*

Yes.

You also mentioned that your husband is now in Stage Two of Alzheimer's and you are concerned because he is getting to be a bit more than you can handle. This is not to say you do not love him, because you do, tremendously. But the reality is that you care for him enough to ensure he has the best of care and help in dealing with his Alzheimer's, is that correct?

Yes, it is.

Mrs. Smith, the next step at this point in time is for you to come in for a visit so you can meet our staff, sample our food, and interact with our residents. What would work better—tomorrow, or even this afternoon?

I can do this afternoon.

Great, would three or four o'clock work better for you?

Three would be great.

Will Mr. Smith be coming too, or just yourself?

Actually, it will be my daughter Mary and myself.

Okay. I look forward to meeting you, Mrs. Smith, and please, don't feel bad. You really are making the right choice by seeing what your options are. By the way, would you mind if I called Mary to introduce myself and put her mind at ease, since she is coming with you? Of course I will follow up with you, but I would just like to make the most of your time here and a quick introduction allows visitors to be much more at ease when they arrive.

Okay, sure. Her number is 888.8823.

Thanks, Mrs. Smith. I'll see you today at 3:00.

THE OPTIONAL CLOSE

Notice that I gave Mrs. Smith options until there were none left. This makes it easy for people to say yes. It has also been proven that people will pick the second option over the first more often. Be sure to have the option you want them to choose as the second one.

WHY THE OPTIONAL CLOSE?

Using an optional close is critical to your success. If you're like most of us, you have salespeople calling every day. The next time this happens, listen closely. Salespeople always close by using a statement that requires a yes or no answer. This is insane, because there is a 50% chance the prospect will say no. Why give this option, if you do not want the prospect to choose it? If no is not a choice, then there is less opportunity for them to say it.

What you want to do instead is offer a choice of two options from which they can choose, both of which will leave you in a good position. Whenever going for any kind of close, ask yourself, "What two options can I give this person?" Using the optional close is a learned process, so do not get discouraged. The more you use it, the easier it will get. The reward for you is that you will close a much higher percentage of sales by using this closing strategy.

HERE ARE SOME OPTIONAL CLOSE EXAMPLES:

- ❏ Would it be best for me to call you back on Monday or would Tuesday work better for you?

❏ Do you have more questions, or would you like to go ahead and leave a deposit to secure the apartment you love?

❏ When might work best for a visit? I can come to you or you can come experience our community firsthand.

As you can see, each option gives you the opportunity to close in some way. Whether your close is simply setting a follow-up date to talk or asking for the deposit, a choice makes the decision much easier. Yes or no is just too final. As you well know, when selling you will not always close on the first attempt. There will be many occasions where you will need to schedule a follow-up call or the next action step. If you do not close, but do schedule a follow-up step, then consider your close a success. In our business, closing is really a series of small action steps taking place over time. It is critically important that you put your foot on the pedal and move people forward in the sales process at all times. Do not wait for them to tell you what's next.

CONFIDENCE PAYS

It is also critical that you speak with confidence. If you're not excited, how can you possibly get them to feel a sense of urgency? Be passionate, express your concerns, tell them what happens next, and they will act much faster.

REPEATING NEEDS

When repeating needs, speak from your heart, in your own

words, as you summarize what you heard the prospect say. This will not only bring clarity to the inquirer, but to you also as you begin to plan the personal visit.

THE POWER OF THE CLOSE

A great client of mine, IntegraCare, has used my sales systems for years. When I first started training in our industry, their sales counselors would send me recorded sales calls (with their side of the conversations only). I would critique each part of the 5-Step Phone System (which we will discuss later in this book) on outbound follow-up calls, and the use of the full Connection Sheet on incoming calls. They became masters of my systems.

I recall speaking last year with Loriann Putzier, the COO, who mentioned that their overall conversions had suddenly dropped. Concerned and committed to high performance from her team, Loriann investigated the decline further and, upon reviewing mystery shops, found that many sales counselors had stopped repeating the needs back in their close. It sounds crazy that something so simple could have such an adverse impact on closing, but it did. Their ratios had dropped by about 15%. Upon identifying where the breakdown in the system was, Loriann addressed it with her team and they immediately began recapping conversations again prior to utilizing the optional close. It was amazing how quickly the conversions shot back up.

This was a great exercise for me and confirmed even more strongly the necessity of reinforcing what prospects identify to be important to them about a prospective move. By repeating the needs back, it proves that you did not just ask lots of great questions, but that you actually listened. This assures prospects that you really do care about them! Here is what Loriann had to say about the systems you are learning to use:

"Since implementing Traci's training, we have improved our system-wide inquiry to appointment ratio by 20% and our appointment to move-in ratio by 18%. We are believers in the system and attribute much of our revenue growth, our adult child satisfaction with the move-in decision, and our ability to meet the emotional needs of our residents, to these powerful tools. Each new sales associate gets the opportunity to attend Traci's sales school as an integral part of the training and orientation process."
—Loriann Putzier, COO IntegraCare Corporation

A SYSTEM YOU CAN MEASURE

As you can see from Loriann's comments and the troubleshooting she did when the system broke down, because she was using a system she was able to quickly identify the problem when it arose. Many companies don't recognize there is a problem until it's too late and even when they do, they are not always sure what to do about it. Consequently, people begin to blame things such as the economy, housing market, time of year, weather, and so on. Typically, there is a specific reason why sales are declining. If using a system, rather than "winging it," that breakdown can be identified quickly and rectified.

Whether making follow-up calls and looking at your contact to appointment conversion, or taking inquiry calls and reviewing your inquiry to appointment conversion, the use of these systems will ensure that you are doing it with mastery and allow you to correct it when it goes off track.

Now that you have a handle on the Adult Child Inquiry Connection Sheet and the close, try a role-play with the Prospective Resident Connection Sheet. These are very similar, yet customized to the prospective resident you are speaking with. As you can see, there is nothing more powerful than identifying needs to build value in regard to your community. If you really want people to come visit, there must be something in it for them.

EXERCISE:

Role-play the Prospect Connection Sheet.

THE VALUE BUILT MUST OUTWEIGH THE DISCOMFORT FELT IF YOU EXPECT PEOPLE TO COME VISIT YOUR COMMUNITY.

The only way you can build more value is to ask more questions. If people say, "No," when you attempt to book an appointment, don't take it personally, just remember that the discomfort felt is overshadowing the value built; there's just not enough in it for them to come in. In essence, the grass must be greener on your side of the fence.

When dealing with new prospects, your first sale is just getting them through the door. Build enough value and they will come see you. The second sale is getting them to deposit and schedule a move-in date. The third sale is the move-in itself. As you can imagine, it all comes down to perceived value. To help you, I have more incredible tools. Before introducing them to you, let's first talk about the personal visit.

A FEW THINGS THAT ARE PROBABLY ON YOUR MIND

Before moving into the visit experience, I want to address a few concerns that are probably on your mind.

First, I want to reiterate that the goal of the inquiry call is to simply schedule an appointment. For many reading this book, that will be a revelation. Believe it or not, many people, perhaps yourself included, are trying to do way too much on the first inquiry call.

You cannot possibly pre-qualify and determine who will and who won't buy via a ten-minute phone call. Give yourself the freedom to simply connect with inquirers and learn what it is they are looking for. Although this sounds incredibly easy, the fact is, it's tough to do. It's tempting to simply talk and sell, and oh so hard to just be still and listen. Again, for those of you who are thinking this book is a bit basic and for newcomers, odds are you are not doing the most basic of all things, which is asking lots of great, open-ended questions and listening to what it is people have to say. Resist all temptation to pre-qualify inquirers and, instead, dig, dig, dig! The Connection Sheets will allow you to accomplish more in less time than you are doing by winging it. If you conducted the exercises outlined in this chapter, you know that by now.

PRICING

I realize that it is incredibly difficult to spend time on the phone with someone when you don't even know if he or she can afford what you are selling. But I would not ask you to do anything I don't do myself. The fact is, people who have money act like they have none and those who have none act like they have a lot. It's impossible to try and determine who can afford your community without taking the time to ask lots of questions, listen, connect, and earn trust from your prospects so they can be honest with you.

If you attempt to pre-qualify, you run the risk of turning your prospects off and losing them forever. If you practice patience and follow the system as outlined, that risk is gone. Again, red flags will come up and in those cases, you refer the prospects where they need to go and move on.

When people ask about pricing information, attempt to redirect them by getting permission to ask a few quick questions. Ninety-five percent of the time, people will become so immersed in the conversation that they will forget to ask again and, instead, schedule an appointment to come in so you can discuss price in person. If they ask a second time, then go there and give a price range based on what you have learned so far. Avoid going into penalties, fees, and other details that can be addressed once the prospect is on site. Keep in mind that this information can be overwhelming to people who are unfamiliar with our industry.

WHAT ABOUT THE ECONOMY?

Every lead is a hot lead; otherwise you would not have received a call. It doesn't matter what's happening economically or what season it is. This means that those who are calling you right now are serious and have a real need. Just because they don't openly share it, doesn't mean it's not there. It's your job to have the skill to draw out the true needs. While your prospects may say that they don't plan to move for another year or two, I would caution you not to take that at face value. Odds are, when they find the community that can deliver on the very things they are looking for, they will move.

Stop focusing on the economy, the time of year, or cyclical trends. Instead, focus on what it is you do want. You can't control the economy, but you can control the conversations you have with people looking to make a move. Eliminate all excuses and remember: this individual called you. If you can show that your community is a fit, the inquirer will come in for a visit. If you can't, they won't; it's that simple.

OBJECTIONS

I will discuss objections in detail as I get into follow-up, so hang in there!

CHAPTER **4**

THE VISIT EXPERIENCE SYSTEM

What if two prospects walked in the door today who were each willing to hand over a check for $80,000, a total of $160,000 (average rent of $40,000 per year, at a two-year length of stay, for example purposes)? The reason for the check? They are so excited about your community that they have chosen to pre-pay for two years. Imagine!

However, to get the checks, you have to get them excited enough to buy. What would you do? How would you make an impact? Let me add in one more element: they are visiting five of your toughest competitors as well. How certain are you that you would be the one to get the checks?

PREPARATION MEETS OPPORTUNITY

In my experience in working with thousands of sales counselors over the past two decades, I can tell you with confidence that most (99%) do not prepare in any way, shape, or form for their appointments. This means that in the exercise I just presented, it would be a random gamble as to who would get the checks. Based on my research, no one person would take the time to prepare in a way that would ensure a victory over the competition.

Sadly, many sales counselors rely on their personalities and "beautiful" communities to do the selling for them. Don't have a renovated community? Then you are left with pure personality. Don't get me wrong, this is a people business and I am a firm believer that people don't really buy the community; they are buying you and the promise you have made as to what life will be like once there. Yet in this day and age, personality is just not enough.

I would say that a strong presence and personality will get you to budget, but not to full occupancy. If you want to experience zero lost revenue days, you must be willing to rely on solid sales systems that eliminate any chance of not getting the sale. If you were in the running to earn the business of our two prospects wanting to pre-pay for two years, you would be certain to earn their business because you literally have every stage of the sales process mapped out, leaving nothing to chance!

Here's the thing: every day you hold appointments with people willing to hand over $80,000, at a minimum! Instead of paying up front, they simply pay over two years (depending on their length of stay). True? The average resident spends $40,000 per year on Assisted Living and stays anywhere from eighteen months to three years. Odds are that you have about eight to ten appointments per week. The best part? They are with hot leads!

Prior to senior housing, I never worked in an industry where hot leads called in every day. I always had to teach people how to go out and cultivate leads, make cold calls, and really do the hard work of getting prospects to express interest. You have the benefit of people calling or walking in because they want what you have. If you've been in sales elsewhere, you know exactly what I am talking about. This is a sales professional's dream. The question is, are you fully taking advantage of this unique opportunity?

PROACTIVE VERSUS REACTIVE

Here's one of our industry's greatest challenges: sales counselors are not proactive.

Let's consider a few examples:

- ❏ They show up for appointments without any knowledge of what their prospects are really looking for. In short, they may know what made them come in, but little else. There is no knowledge of what's most important, what it was about the ad that spoke to them, who the decision makers are, what their greatest concerns are, and so on. This goes right back to the sales counselors assuming that if they can form a relationship during the appointment, the prospects will be so excited, they will buy. Not true!

- ❏ They don't attempt to close on the next step, but instead request that the prospect call when they are ready to make a decision. The fact is that they are scared and are not going to willingly do anything until someone prompts them to do so.

- ❏ They don't ask for a second contact number or e-mail address, which makes follow-up next to impossible. How many people are sitting at home by their phones?

❏ They wait seven to ten days following an on-site visit to follow up with prospects. In seven to ten days, they might have already moved in elsewhere. It is important to follow up immediately, while people are in the shopping mode and interested (more on this in the chapter on follow-up)!

❏ They don't attempt to drill down and really learn the details about a prospect until they realize it's too late and they've lost the prospect's interest. Once they realize the prospect is about to deposit at a competitor's, they jump all over it.

I personally don't believe sales counselors intend to be reactive. Yet, truth be told, the majority of sales professionals across all industries operate in a very reactive manner. This is why less than ten percent actually thrive in sales. It's also important to remember that salespeople are not born, they are made. We have to teach people what it means to be proactive, why it's so important to the sales process, and the impact it can make on people's lives. In short, they have to learn. Let's start with those critical appointments.

FROM A TOUR TO A VISIT EXPERIENCE

We must stop using the word tour. If you desire to simply hold "tours," then so be it. I consider tours a kind of show-and-tell model. Our savvy buyers want more. If you can move from conducting a standard tour to creating a visit experience, you will see the length of your sales cycle dramatically decline. The better experience someone has at your community, the more likely he or she will be to return and experience more. Clo͜ ͜ ͜g today is a series of small steps and "mini-closes." It's important that we create a great first experience so we can hook them and get them to come back for another experience—a dining experience, weekend stay, Friday night cocktail party, golf outing, gardening event, and so on. Going forward, think: experience!

My appointment strategy is very simple. Following through on it will prove difficult. It's not that what I'm about to share is hard, but that it takes time and that happens to be one of your most precious resources. Before I share any training, I want you to think logically. The more time you invest up front, preparing for the visit, the greater success you will have. Knowledge without action is of little use. What good would it be to learn about the needs of your prospects and then not act on them during the course of the visit? Unfortunately, very few people really get this. Due to hectic schedules, they intend to plan out a great visit, get side-tracked, and before they know it, the family is on-site. The result is the same standard tour that is given to everyone.

Keep in mind that what made the prospect come in was the perceived value. The prospect was convinced you could meet the stated needs. If you don't demonstrate that on the visit, your guest may leave disgruntled and feeling misled.

PERSONAL VISIT SYSTEM

❑ Pre-plan the personal visit prior to the family showing up.

❑ Customize the visit to match the needs of the family.

❑ Answer questions.

- ❏ Use "the scale" to gauge closing potential.

- ❏ Close.

- ❏ Schedule the next action step.

Success is about preparation meeting opportunity!

PRE-PLAN THE PERSONAL VISIT

Upon completing the Connection Sheet, we suggest that you immediately determine your appointment strategy to ensure you don't give a canned tour. The key to much of your success and this training is being proactive.

Based on the needs identified ask, "What are my priorities?" Demonstrate on the visit you can meet the needs of the inquirer and you will be one step closer to getting a deposit. At the appointment, your objective is to build enough value to get a deposit that day, if at all possible. This is your key objective.

If, for example, you talk to an adult child whose number one concern is her mother's safety and her number two concern is her social environment, then you would put safety as one and social as two. Then you would need to strategize what you can do that will impact the visitor and demonstrate that you can not only meet, but exceed, their expectations. See an example of this below.

EXAMPLE:

- ❏ You may call your director of nursing and tell her that you would like for her to spend five minutes with a family coming in to discuss what measures she and her staff take to protect people from hazards to their safety.

❏ You then call your activities director and tell her that socialization is very important to the visitor and request that she also join you on the appointment for an overview of things that Mom can do upon moving in that are pre-planned and customized to her personal needs. If you determined that Mom was an avid gardener prior to the death of her husband, you might have the activities director show her the garden and share how the residents are involved in planting, weeding, and nurturing flowers. She may even go as far as to have a resident working on the garden who can in turn talk to the family as a third party endorsement. The activities director can then provide the family with a schedule, highlighted with key events she feels the mother would enjoy.

CUSTOM HOME OR TRACT HOME?

If you had the choice to purchase a new home, would you prefer to move into a custom home or a tract home? Odds are that you said custom. Who wouldn't? We want visiting families to feel the same way, as if your community was made for their loved one, but you can't do this if you don't pre-plan and strategize ways to make this happen!

CUSTOMIZE THE VISIT TO MATCH THE NEEDS OF THE FAMILY

Once you have done the pre-planning, all you have to do is follow through. Guests visiting your community should feel important, valued, and as though you really want them or their loved ones to live there. All the things you pre-planned should make a tremendous impact and leave a lasting impression. Again, strategy is key here. If it's a walk-in and there is no time to strategize, do the best you can to customize. If it's a home or hospital visit, again, be creative and customize the literature provided and the time spent as much as possible.

ANSWER QUESTIONS

This is pretty self-explanatory. Of course you want to see if the person you are visiting with has any questions. What's important here is that you answer them as honestly as you can. It does no good to land a sale and then have someone turn around and move out thirty days later. If the questions make you realize that it's not a fit, then let the visitor know. Save the prospect and yourself the headache of making the wrong decision.

USE THE SCALE TO GAUGE CLOSING POTENTIAL

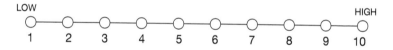

Prior to going for a close, it's critical that you insert the following question right before asking for the check:

> *Mrs. Smith, on a scale of 1-10, with 10 being the highest, what's your level of interest in our community right now?*

If she says, "Well, I would say a 7," you should respond with, "What would make it a 10?"

This question is very powerful. It is direct and allows people to be honest in their answers without feeling like they are going to hurt your feelings. We have been testing this question for some time with our coaching students and it's incredibly powerful. The most important thing it will do is provide clarity. You will know exactly where your prospect stands, instead of simply guessing. Prospects will feel good because this question forces them to really think about where they are on the scale, and what needs to happen to make the community more of a fit.

WHAT WOULD MAKE IT A 10?

When you ask, "What would make it a 10?" you will hear a variety of answers. Some of the time you can move the prospect up on the scale, and some of the time it's out of your hands. What matters is that you will be able to accurately categorize each prospect as a hot, warm, or cold lead, and better manage your follow-up.

SOME TYPICAL RESPONSES

- ❏ I just need more time to think about it. We just started our search this week. There is nothing you personally can do.

- ❏ I really want a two-bedroom and all you have is a one-bedroom.

- ❏ I have noticed that people are just sitting around. I am looking for more of an active lifestyle.

In example number one, "I just need more time to think about it," you know it's a matter of follow-up. Of course, you can and should ask a few more probing, open-ended questions to move them to action.

In example number two, "I really want a two-bedroom and all you have is a one-bedroom," you have the opportunity to build value and create urgency in regard to moving today versus tomorrow. What you want to do is highlight the value your community will bring, while minimizing the pain of temporarily living in a one-bedroom. If you really want the prospect to move, the value *must* exceed the pain. There must be more in it for someone to live there now in a smaller unit, than to stay at home. You might say something like:

> *You mentioned that you stay in most of the time, Mrs. Smith, but that when your husband was alive you were always doing something. Whether it was planting flowers, attending a garden club meeting, or just going to dinner and a movie, you were on the go. Is that correct?*

> *Yes...*

> *You also mentioned that since he passed, you have become more withdrawn, and you feel isolated and lonely. In talking to you, I get the sense that this is not your personality and that you desire much more; you want a full life again.*

> *Yes, that's correct.*

> *What I would like to suggest, Mrs. Smith, is that you consider temporarily moving into a one-bedroom apartment. You will be in a smaller space, but the objective is to have you outside of that*

space as much as possible—attending events, socializing, garden-ing, and more. We want to help you regain your quality of life. Of course, our end goal will be to move you to the first available two-bedroom when it comes up. Is this something you would consider, or would you perhaps like to take a look at a few one-bedrooms first?

Again, the goal is to get the value to exceed the pain. Mrs. Smith may have to compromise, but her overall quality of life will be better as a result.

OVERCOMING OBJECTIONS

Please note that we are not overcoming objections. We are solving problems and presenting alternate opportunities. I do not believe in overcoming objections. You want to focus people on what they want versus what they don't. With the systems I have introduced, objections will become a thing of the past and problem-solving and value building will assume their place.

IT'S A 10! THE CLOSE

If a prospect says she's at a 10 on the scale, then great! Ask for the deposit. Just as I taught you earlier, repeat the needs back and, without hesitation, go into an optional close.

EXAMPLE:

Mrs. Smith, based on everything you told me, it sounds like you really want to move out of your home. It's too big for you and, most importantly, it's a constant reminder of the past and is causing you tremendous sorrow. Instead of living for tomorrow, all you can think about is yesterday, is this correct?

Yes...

You also mentioned that what's most important to you is a community that has a lot going on socially. You want a community that is innovative in its programming and that has more of a youthful environment. Based on what you need and what we have, it really seems like a great fit!

I know you really liked our garden view apartment due to the roses, and I love that one too. You also seemed excited about our lake view. It's a tough choice, but which would you prefer to make a deposit on, so we can hold it for you and begin discussing what's next?

THEN PAUSE. DON'T SAY A WORD: HE WHO SPEAKS FIRST LOSES!

This is where many people get nervous and start literally talking people out of the sale. *Let the prospect speak.* She will either pick from the two options or object. The great news is, the odds are in your favor. You already know you are a 10 on the scale. In reality, all you had to do was ask.

If by chance the prospect does object, then ask more questions.

EXAMPLE:

If Mrs. Smith says, "I'm just not ready to make that kind of commitment today," you need to ask more open-ended questions, such as:

What is going to change about your situation between today and next week that will really make a difference regarding this decision?

or

What in particular is causing you to hesitate on this decision?

If you are thinking it, then ask. You have to be direct and delve deeply if you want to be successful.

ACTION ITEM

Grab an index card. Write the scale question down and keep it handy on all visits for the next thirty days. Practice makes perfect, and I want you to learn it the right way.

SCHEDULE THE NEXT ACTION STEP

No matter what happens, whether you get the check or not, you must define what happens next. Rarely do we see salespeople do this. I don't know why—this is the easy part—but salespeople rarely bring closure to the visit. I call this step "closing the loop." Doing this clarifies for the prospect what to expect next.

YOU GET A DEPOSIT

If you get a deposit, the sale does not end here. You need the move-in to happen, too. Clearly define what happens next and make it exciting. More importantly, follow through on what you say is going to happen next. Don't assume they know—verbalize it.

YOU DON'T GET A DEPOSIT

If you do not get a deposit, be certain to let the visitor know when you will follow up. Close the loop! Many times, the prospect will say, "I just need to think about it. I'll call you in a few days." Come on, they are being polite. Even if they mean it, rarely will someone follow up with you. People are not excited about this decision. They are overwhelmed with fear, guilt, and second thoughts. You need to let them know when they can expect to hear from you, no matter what. Consider the example below.

EXAMPLE OF CLOSING THE LOOP

Mrs. Smith, if I don't hear from you by the end of the week, do you mind if I just touch base to make sure you don't have any questions?

That's all you have to do; now the loop is closed. You may go on to ask if morning or afternoon is better and if she has a cell phone, but other than that, schedule the call in your contact manager and follow through. If you don't follow up, odds are you will not get a move-in. He who wants and courts the sale will earn it. Did you know that 80% of all sales close after the fifth call? This is just the beginning.

ASK FOR A SECOND CONTACT NUMBER AND E-MAIL ADDRESS

Be sure to ask for alternate phone number and the prospect's e-mail address. Rarely will you reach people at home. Two numbers provide you with an increased opportunity to follow up properly. Because a multimedia approach is important, you also want to obtain as many e-mail addresses as possible. I have found that, while people fail to return my phone calls, they almost always return my e-mails. Pay close attention to who prefers phone calls and who prefers e-mails (or texts), and communicate with them in the manner they favor.

THE HOME

It's time to get to some of your most pressing concerns. I imagine you consistently get the objection: I need to sell my house. If you are an entry fee community, this is more than likely your number one obstacle to closing sales. Let's use this opportunity to learn to think differently. Relax and open your mind to possibilities that perhaps you have not yet considered. Start by saying, "If it's not the collapse of the stock market yesterday" or "I'm not ready yet" today, it will always be something.

I have been selling since I was seven years old and, whether it was knocking on doors to sell homemade tissue boxes and Christmas wreaths, life insurance, or training services, there have always been objections in my selling career—and there always will be.

There are two things we as sales professionals ask of our prospects that they simply don't want to part with—their time or their money. Think about it. You are either asking someone for an appointment or a check. That, my friend, is the nature of sales. For your prospects, these are two of their most precious resources. You must get used to "the game" of sales. You attempt to close and your prospect objects. To be successful, you not only must get used to this, you must have a system to handle it. Objections are your prospect's way of saying, "I don't see the value in what it is you are trying to get me to do."

Rather than telling you what they are really thinking ("I don't like it here," or "There are a bunch of old people sleeping in your lobby and I'm not that old"), they will say something like, "You know, I really need to sell my home first," or "I need more time to consider all our options." Sound familiar? What you need to do is the following:

1. Relate. Say something like, "I understand."

2. Ask more questions to get prospects focused on what they want.

RELATE

Relating to people and acknowledging that you understand them is very important. The last thing people want to deal with is a pushy salesperson who seems to have all the answers. They want someone who understands them and can see their point of view. By using a statement such as "I understand," prospects can relax and lower their guard. This also gives you a moment to recover and come up with a great open-ended question to ask.

ASK MORE OPEN-ENDED QUESTIONS

You will notice that when you say, "I understand," the body language or tone of voice of your prospects will change and be more relaxed. In their minds, you get them, and that feels good. You want to either get permission to ask a few more questions or just start asking them. I am going to go into objections in great detail during the follow-up and closing chapters. However, I didn't want to close out this chapter on the visit experience without addressing just a few objections, such as selling a home.

Remember, you want to establish strong value. If you can get them excited to buy, they will be more likely to take those first steps and put their home on the market. If they are not even willing to do that, you are nowhere near building the value necessary to get them to deposit and move in. Here are some great probing questions to ask when discussing the sale of a home:

- ❏ May I ask when you plan to put your home on the market?

- ❏ Have you interviewed realtors yet?

- ❏ What kind of information have you been able to obtain regarding listing prices or comps in the area?

- ❏ As we talk today, what are the next steps for you in moving this process forward and to getting your home on the market?

I realize that many of your prospects will say that they are going to wait to sell their homes in order to make repairs or renovate with the hope of a higher listing price, but let's be realistic. Odds are, this is not the real barrier. My question to you is, if your prospects are going to wait to sell their homes, why are they calling you now? I firmly believe that they call because they have a pressing need, even if you sell for a CCRC, Life Care, or an Independent Living community. If someone were going to wait for home prices to rise, realistically they would not be calling you now. Yes, I realize some people do plan their lives out well in advance, but most don't. This means you have a real opportunity to drill down and discover what's really going on so you can help them move forward.

YOU WILL KNOW

When a prospect puts a home on the market and begins taking the steps necessary to move in, you will know he is serious. If he won't take this very important first step, he simply does not see the value yet. In this case, you are back to square one. Ask yourself:

- ❏ What is the underlying core need here?

- ❏ What underlying fears are standing between the visit and making the decision to move?

- ❏ What concerns have I not addressed?

- ❏ Have I communicated with all decision makers and influencers?

- ❏ Are there more resources or tools I can use to put minds at ease?

MOST IMPORTANT CLOSING STEP

It is important to remember, *you must proactively schedule the next action step.* If done before the prospect leaves the building, you have succeeded. Just because she didn't buy today, does not mean she won't buy tomorrow. You have to be her advocate, her counselor, and the one to get her excited to buy!

CHAPTER 5

THE FOLLOW-UP AND CLOSING SYSTEMS

Did you know? Eighty percent of all sales close after the *fifth* call, and ninety percent of all sales professionals quit following up after the *fourth* call!

FOLLOW-UP IN OUR INDUSTRY STINKS

Here are the facts. Follow-up is not happening in any capacity in our industry. If you want to know why your building is not full, I am certain that follow-up is a big part of the problem.

If you are a sales counselor, you may disagree. To make sure we are all on the same page, please humor me and conduct the following exercise.

1. Pull five leads at random and print their history. These should be people who have inquired in the last ninety days. It's probably best if they are warm leads.

2. Once you have the leads printed out and in front of you, notate the following:

- How many days passed between the first visit and the first follow-up call?

- How many days passed between the first follow-up call and the second follow-up call or task that occurred?

- How many days from the second task to the third task that actually occurred?

As you can see, I am assuming that the first follow-up call did occur. Sadly, this very important step does not happen at the majority of communities in our industry. If you don't agree, we can just agree to disagree. In my opinion, it's an epidemic and one of the reasons so many apartments are sitting empty. In my research, I have found the length of time from the first visit to the follow-up call to be seven days at minimum. The second to the third, if it happens at all, will be another ten to fourteen days. The third task, for those sales counselors who do aggressive follow-up? Another thirty days!

PUT THIS IN PERSPECTIVE

A hot lead calls, wanting to possibly buy what you have to offer. He takes his valuable time to come in and visit your community (and more than likely, four or five of your competitors' properties also). Seven days after visiting, the prospect gets a follow-up call that goes something like this, "Hi, Mrs. Smith, it's Traci from the Whispering Pines. How are you?"

Number one, Mrs. Smith has no clue who you are and, while she recalls the name, she can't even remember the location of Whispering Pines. It's been too long and she has been many places since visiting you. Number two, she is regretting answering the phone because she realizes you are calling from one of the many places she has looked, and she is burnt out and exhausted. She may have even convinced herself that, in fact, she really doesn't need to move.

I'm certain you have experienced this very situation many times in the past. To be unforgettable, you have to do something that earns you that right. This means providing service unlike anything the prospect has encountered while shopping for a community, creating an on-site visit experience that was not only memorable but emotionally impacting, and last but not least, following up *immediately*—ideally, the same day of the prospect's visit. Don't panic, I will share more on this in a moment, and trust me, you will see results and buy into it quickly if I can get you to do it.

The point I am trying to make, and will reinforce throughout this chapter, is that you must raise the bar on follow-up expectations. This chapter will outline what tools to use and what language works when making calls. Yet you must begin making more follow-up calls and commit to the long haul when working with leads, if you expect to fill up your community. Following up just once or twice, when you have the time, is not going to work. You need a turnkey follow-up system and a daily call time blocked out in your calendar if you expect to achieve zero lost revenue days!

The TRACI BILD 5-Step Phone System

I would like to begin by introducing you to a proven 5-Step Phone System that will assist you in booking one appointment out of every second contact made. This very system has been time-tested for over twenty years, across all industries. When used correctly, it will ensure you have a full calendar and permanently eliminate any call reluctance and fear of the telephone you may currently have. I recommend that you purchase some index cards and a recorder to master this process. Upon mastering it, you will move into the top percentage of sales professionals who sell senior housing within our industry—selling ten or more apartments a month!

If you don't want to be treated like a salesperson, then it is critical that you don't sound like one. Eighty-five percent of sales success stems from relationships formed. The 5-Step Phone System is designed to aid you in establishing an immediate connection and relationship with people inquiring about your community. Although it may not be easy to change your method of selling, or follow-up in particular, you will find the rewards of this system to be well worth your efforts. When learning to use the five steps, it is critical that you do the following:

❏ Use the 5-Step System on all outbound calls.

❏ Never pre-judge whom you should use the system with.

❏ Stay focused on one step at a time.

❏ Organize your calls (returning inquiry calls, follow-up calls, referral source calls, etc.).

❏ Notice and practice phrases that work for you.

"Keep an open attitude and be willing to try new things."
–Arthur Martinez, CEO Sears Roebuck

Sears lost $3.9 billion in 1992, but under the first year of Arthur's guidance, earned over $1 billion!

EXERCISE:

In the space provided, write the following sentence with the hand you normally write with:

Hello, my name is _____

(your name) and I am a(n) _____

(Admission Director, etc.) with _____

_____

_____

Now, write the same sentence with your opposite hand, the one you never write with. Don't give up! Be patient and write until the sentence is complete.

_____

_____

_____

_____

How did that make you feel? Were you frustrated, angry, or annoyed? More than likely it was not an enjoyable experience. Yet I am certain that with much practice you could learn to write with your other hand...if you had the right motivation to do so.

Just as writing with your left hand, if you are right-handed, was frustrating, it will be frustrating to learn new success habits. The phone system you are about to learn is not hard—just different and something you have never done before. If you want to reach your desired level of occupancy (100%), maintain it, then exceed it by building a solid wait list or driving your rent up, all while learning to work smart, not hard, then *you must become a telephone professional.* The 5-Step Phone System you are about to learn will help you do just that!

IMPORTANT SUCCESS TIPS

❏ Use the following system on 100% of your outbound calls.

❏ Notice and practice phrases that work well for you.

❏ Focus on what is different about this system that is different from what you have done before in sales.

❏ Realize that this system is built around the importance of establishing relationships and creating value in the eyes of the potential resident and his or her family members.

"Consumers are Statistics. Customers are People."
—Stanley Marcus, Chairman Emeritus, Neiman-Marcus

5-STEP PHONE PROCESS OVERVIEW FOR OUTBOUND CALLS

Your objective is to:

1. Obtain a simple response

Getting a simple response gets people involved in the conversation, slowly but surely. Ninety-nine percent of the time, they will respond with a "Yes." The following are examples of other simple responses you may get.

"Hi."	"Hello."
"Yes."	"Do I know you?"
"Who?"	"How are you?"

To get a simple response, use the following statement:

Hello, _____, this is _____ calling.
       (first name only)   (your first and last name)

PAUSE.

IMPORTANT: *Before going into the opening step, confirm you have the right person on the telephone by saying, "Hello, may I speak with_____?" Once you know you're talking to the person you want, then start this telephone process with the Opening, Step One.*

When opening your call, it's important that you trust the system. We have proven that when opening in the following manner you will get a "yes" response 99% of the time. When starting your call, be sure to ask for the person you're calling. If at all possible, ask for the prospect by *first name*; it sets the tone for a personable conversation. If you ask for Mrs. Ester Jones (unless the prospect has specifically requested you to), the individual will become guarded or armed. Remember, we are trying to establish a relationship. Once confirmed that you are talking to the right person, start with Step One. Here is an example:

Hi, is Jack in?

This is he...

STEP ONE

Hi Jack, this is Traci Bild calling.

Yes?

IMPORTANT SUCCESS TIPS

- ❏ Use the prospect's name in the opening.

- ❏ It is critical that you identify yourself by both first and last names.

- ❏ Do not reveal the name of the company you are with yet. Identifying yourself (with both first and last names) in the opening, instead of your company, allows you to form an immediate relationship, so the prospect will not feel threatened.

- ❏ Be certain that you use the word "calling" after your name, or you will not get a "yes" response.

- ❏ You must pause after the word *calling*. If you don't, how can the prospect possibly say, "Yes?"

TAKE A MOMENT TO PRACTICE YOUR OPENING STEP:

Write it out in the space provided.

_____

_____

_____

_____

THINGS TO LOOK FOR:

- ❏ Did you include the prospect's name in your opening?

- ❏ Did you include both your first and last names?

- ❏ Did you use the word *calling* after your name?

TRY IT AGAIN

Take a moment to say the Opening Step out loud several times. It's important that you get comfortable with this step. Although it is easy to do, psychologically it is much different than what you may be used to. By nature, salespeople want to talk and talk. Throughout this training, you will find that it is much more effective if you learn to listen, starting at the beginning of the call with the Opening.

Hello, _____, this is _____ calling.

PAUSE.

POSSIBLE RESPONSES YOU MAY RECEIVE

When using the Opening Step, you will get a "yes" response approximately 99% of the time. What a great way to start your call! Again, the word *calling* empowers prospects to respond with a "yes." Other possible responses you may get are:

❏   Who?

❏   Do I know you?

❏   A long, uncomfortable pause...

If the prospect responds by saying, *"Who?"* simply repeat your first and last names and pause again. If the pause continues, then move immediately to Step Two, Disarming. If the prospect says, *"Do I know you?"* or says nothing, move on to the Disarming step as well.

The important thing to remember is, if you don't get a yes initially, most of the time you will go on to the Disarming step where you will get two yes responses, so please have patience! The only time you will not move on to Disarming is if the person says, "Who?" In this case, you will repeat your name, then move on to Step Two, Disarming.

PAUSING WILL ALLOW YOU TO ENGAGE PROSPECTS IN THE CONVERSATION

IMPORTANT SUCCESS TIPS

❏ When opening, you will find it difficult to pause after saying the word *calling*. If you have to, count to three, then move on. Pausing effectively will pay off in the form of a yes—keep in mind that anytime you get too uncomfortable or don't know what to do, just move on to Step Two.

❏ If you have spoken with the prospect several times and are 100% certain that he knows who you are and you're on a first name basis, then you can eliminate your last name and just say, "Hi, John, it's Traci calling!" More than likely, he will respond in a very positive way such as, "Hi, Traci!"

❏ *Never ask*, "How are you?" This is one phrase that takes you out of control of the call. If the prospect says, "How are you?" reply positively and move on to the next step. This is not rude; it's smart and will keep your call moving forward in the direction you want it to go. As you will see, the entire call is built around the prospect and is completely focused on his or her needs.

*"Do not fear mistakes. Wisdom is often
born of... mistakes."*
–Paul Galvin

2 Disarming

Your objective is to:

1. Get a "yes" response and obtain permission to talk

In this era of frequent telemarketing calls, it has become second nature for people to resist phone solicitation. You can lower or eliminate this resistance by getting the people you call to say YES. In addition, getting a yes response will increase your odds of getting permission to talk.

Getting permission to talk is the only way to ensure the person is listening.

The easiest way to get a yes response is to start your sentence with one of these phrases:

I understand... OR

If you recall...

THE POWER OF YES!

As an individual who sells senior housing services, it is impor-tant that you build an immediate connection with prospects. The last thing you want to do is be perceived as annoying. It is proven that the more yes responses you get, the more posi-tive "state of mind" the prospects will go into as the conversa-tion moves forward. Because of constant solicitations at home and work, people are naturally guarded and resist talking with people they feel are trying to sell them something, even if they initially inquired about you.

In most cases, each time a salesperson calls the prospect, he or she pretty much sounds the same—usually something like, "Hi, Mr. Jones, this is Keith Clark with Rolling Hills Assist-ed Living. The reason I'm calling you today is..." and from this point forward the salesperson rambles on and on. Does this sound familiar? How many solicitation calls do you get at home that sound like this? It is a sad but true fact: everyone sells the same. Because everyone sells the same, they sound the same—like a salesperson—and prospects run the other way!

The objective of the 5-Step Phone System is *not* to sound or act like a solicitor or salesperson but, instead, to disarm the prospect and engage her in meaningful conversation. Once engaged, the objective is to identify what needs the person has that you can offer solutions to. The system you are learning is designed to help you obtain three yes responses in the first minute of the call. What this does is the following:

❏ Puts the prospect you are calling in a positive state of mind

❏ Engages the prospect in the conversation

❏ Ensures you are in control of the call, not the prospect

- ❏ Helps establish a personal connection and relationship with the prospect

- ❏ Gives the prospect an idea of why you are calling

- ❏ Confirms the prospect has the time to talk with you

- ❏ Makes the call enjoyable for you to conduct

SO HOW DO YOU GET THE NEXT TWO YES RESPONSES?

When in Step Two, Disarming, you will always start with one of two phrases:

I understand... OR *If you recall...*

If you know something about the person you're calling, you will start this step with "I understand." When using this phrase, you will state a fact about the prospect. Here are some examples:

- ❏ I understand you're looking into Independent Living communities?

- ❏ I understand that you're the business manager for Dr. Goldstein's office?

- ❏ I understand that you're a friend of Sally Mae Smith's?

- ❏ I understand your mother is being discharged from Halifax Medical Center on Friday?

In all of the above examples, you are stating a fact about

the person you are calling. So long as the fact is correct, you will get a "yes" response 100% of the time. This is where you will obtain your second yes.

Much of the time, you will not be stating a fact, but recalling an event of some sort. Start this step with, "If you recall..." Here are some examples:

- ❏ If you recall, you inquired about Burgandy Place this morning?

- ❏ If you recall, you asked me to call you back this week in regard to scheduling a tour of The Meadows?

- ❏ If you recall, you came in for a visit at The Heritage Center on Friday?

- ❏ If you recall, we met at our Spa Day here at Whispering Oaks Retirement Community last week?

Again, "If you recall..." will elicit a yes response from prospects 100% of the time unless the contact is so dated they just don't remember the occurrence. So long as your information is correct, you will get a yes response 100% of the time in the first part of Disarming.

IMPORTANT SUCCESS TIPS

- ❏ When Disarming, always state a fact or recall an event.

- ❏ Pause after this first part of Disarming, or the prospect will not have the opportunity to say yes.

❏ When Disarming, do it in the form of a question. This means that your voice should have a "question" tone to it when recalling the event or stating the fact.

❏ If you have a cold lead, look at the information you do have and ask yourself, "How can I disarm this prospect? What do I know about him?"

❏ Always start this step with either "I understand," or "If you recall."

THE SECOND PART OF DISARMING

After receiving the second yes, move on to the second part of Disarming: obtaining permission to talk. When doing this, say what is comfortable for you. Here are some examples:

❏ Did I catch you at a good time?

❏ Is this a convenient time to talk?

❏ Do you have a quick minute?

You may be tempted not to ask permission to speak because the call is going so well. Many people feel that if they ask, the prospect will in turn say no. However, we have proven time and time again that if you ask, people will respond with a yes. Many times, the prospect will say yes because they respect you for asking for their time before just taking it. Other times, they will say yes because they are curious and add, "What do you want?" You have one final thing working in your favor: the prospect has already said yes two times. She is in the habit of saying yes, which makes it easier to say it again and again. You are successfully putting the prospect in a positive state of mind, she does not feel threatened, and she feels comfortable talking with you. Why wouldn't she say yes?

If for any reason the prospect says, "No, this is not a good time," then respond by saying, "Would an hour from now work better for you?" or "Would this time tomorrow work better for you?" Don't ever ask, "Well, when should I call you back?" People are busy. This type of question will only frustrate them. Additionally, you are handing control of the call over to the prospect. You want to stay in control all the way to the end. Options work great, too. You might say, "Would an hour from now work better or would you just prefer I call you back tomorrow?" Typically, the prospect will pick from one of your options. Oftentimes they will say, "What's this about?" If this is how the prospect responds, then move on to the next step, the Reason.

POSSIBLE RESPONSES TO SEEKING PERMISSION

Yes.
No.
What's this about?

If you don't ask permission to speak, it's like walking in the front door of someone's home without an invitation. Don't assume the prospect wants to talk with you. Use the system, trust it to work for you, and you will find that the prospect will want to talk with you.

#1 WAY TO ASK: We have consistently found that the phrase, "Do you have a quick minute?" earns you the greatest number of yes responses to this timing question.

TRY IT NOW

Take a moment to determine how you would Disarm the following prospects. Write your Disarming statement in the spaces provided.

#1. An inquiry call came in over the weekend and you need to call back and schedule a visit. All you know is the person's name and number, and nothing else. How might you Disarm?

_____

_____

_____

_____

#2. A resident gives you a referral. How might you Disarm the referral?

_____

_____

_____

_____

#3. You are following up on a visit that took place one to two days ago. How might you Disarm the prospect?

_____

_____

_____

_____

#4. You have a lead that is close to a year old. You want to follow up and move the prospect forward in the sales process. How might you Disarm?

_____

_____

_____

_____

Are you getting the hang of it? When Disarming, state a fact or recall an event. If you have the person's name and number, you have to know something about the prospect, which in turn makes this Disarming step possible.

POSSIBLE ANSWERS

Below are some sample Disarming statements you might have used:

#1. An inquiry call came in over the weekend and you need to call back and schedule a visit. All you know is the person's name and number; nothing else. How might you Disarm?

If you recall, you left a message in regard to setting up a visit experience here at Oak Crest Assisted Living Center?

#2. A resident gives you a referral. How might you Disarm the referral?

I understand you're a good friend of Mabel Smith?

#3. You are following up on a visit that took place one to two days ago. How might you Disarm the prospect?

If you recall, I showed you around Maplewood Village on Tuesday?

#4. You have a lead that is close to a year old. You want to follow up and move the prospect forward in the sales process. How might you Disarm?

If you recall, you had inquired about Boca Ciega Bay Retirement Community, oh, about nine months ago?

ONCE YOU HAVE COMPLETED THE OPENING AND THE FIRST PART OF DISARMING YOU WILL HAVE TWO YES RESPONSES. WHAT A GREAT WAY TO START YOUR CALLS!

What do you do after you get the second yes? _____

_____

EXERCISE: _____

TAKE A MOMENT TO WORK THROUGH AN EXERCISE WITH STEPS ONE AND TWO.

You have been working with a family and they are in the decision phase. They are looking at two other communities and must make a decision by the end of the week (they have already toured your community). Using the Opening and Disarming Steps, write out how you would make this call.

OPENING

_____

_____

_____

_____

DISARMING

_____

_____

_____

_____

WHAT DO YOU DO BETWEEN EACH STEP?

_____

_____

_____

_____

Now take a moment and role-play this out loud.

POTENTIAL ANSWERS:

OPENING

Hi, Mrs. Smith, this is Traci Bild calling...

If you know her well and are sure she will recognize you, you can exclude your last name and do the following:

Hi, Mrs. Smith, it's Traci calling...

DISARMING

If you recall, you suggested that I contact you today in regard to a potential move to Forest Ridge...

Depending on your style and success with obtaining permission to speak, you may say, "Do you have just a minute?" If you find prospects typically say no to this timing question, leave it out and go straight to the Reason Step.

BETWEEN EACH STEP YOU WILL: Pause!

NOTE: If, when you open, the prospect says, "How are you?" reply with, "I'm great," or, "Fine, thanks" (your own style), and move into Disarming. There is no reason for you to reply, "Great, how are you?" Doing this may cause you to lose control of your focus and the call. Your goal is to stay on task and get the prospect to commit to your community.

3 The Reason

Your objectives are to:

1. Obtain permission to ask questions

2. State who you're with if not done in Disarming

3. Explain the purpose of your call

4. Be very personable, be caring, be yourself

5. Seek controlled, predictable responses

The bottom line in this step is to seek permission to ask questions. You can't build value if you don't know what the prospect's needs are. You will find that 99% of the people you ask will freely say yes to this question.

EXAMPLE:

The reason I'm calling is, I wanted to thank you for taking the time to come visit us yesterday. I really enjoyed meeting you and your husband, and wondered if I could ask you a couple quick questions about your visit?

If the person says YES, you have accomplished your objective.

The Reason Step is where you will obtain permission to ask questions and learn as much as possible about your prospect. Most people in sales tend to talk a lot. Keep in mind that you can't learn by talking, only by listening. It is in this Reason Step that you will tell the prospect who you are with. You might have done so already in the Disarming Step. If not, it will happen here. Again, the reason you have not done this yet is that you have been working to connect with the prospect, establish rapport, and engage him in meaningful conversation. It has been proven that, psychologically, if you receive three yes responses from a prospect, you will obtain even more as you progress. This is why you have used this strategy up to this point. Psychology is doing much of the work for you!

HOW TO BEGIN

The Reason Step will always start with the following phrase:

The reason I'm calling is...

The Reason Step will always end with:

Permission to ask questions

What goes between the two is a brief statement to personalize the conversation. When telling the prospect why you are calling, be certain that you keep it short and to the point. You have worked hard to engage prospects in the conversation and make them comfortable with you. The last thing you want to do is put them on guard by rambling. It is important to actually have a set reason for calling. It is here in the Reason Step that you will express the reason.

IMPORTANT SUCCESS TIPS

❏ Use the Reason Step to let your personality come through. This is the one place you get to actually talk.

❏ Be certain to use voice inflections. Think of your voice as a musical instrument; you want people to enjoy talking to you. Using inflections means that your voice should go up and down as you speak. In essence, you are making yourself sound interesting.

❏ Mirror the prospect's tone and speed. If the prospect is talking quickly, speed up your voice. If the prospect is talking very slowly, slow down. Doing this will allow the person you are speaking with to better connect with you.

❏ Use the prospect's name. Doing this makes the conversation more personable and people love to hear others say their names.

❏ Be confident. As you explain the purpose of your call, expect success; be proud of the services you are offering.

❏ Wait until this step to tell prospects who you are with.

ON THE FOLLOWING PAGE ARE A VARIETY OF REASON STEPS YOU CAN USE WHEN CALLING ON PROSPECTS

Keep in mind that the 5-Step Phone System is not a script. This means that you do not have to read the Reason Steps verbatim.

Feel free to mix and match the steps below, develop your own reasons, and so on. These are here to offer you guidance. If you want to read the Reason Steps exactly as they are, that is fine too!

Call Back to Book a Visit:

The reason I'm calling is, you had expressed an interest in visiting our community here at Eaglewood and I wondered if I could ask you a few quick questions to see how I can best assist you?

Calling a Referral Given to You by a Resident:

The reason I'm calling is, I'm the Community Relations Director here at The Cove Retirement Center where Mabel lives, and she had mentioned that you were looking into Independent Living communities and suggested I give you a quick call. I was wondering if I could ask you a few quick questions to learn a little bit more about what you might be looking for?

Following Up on a Recent Tour:

The reason I'm calling is, I wanted to thank you for coming to take a look at The Pines on Monday. I really enjoyed meeting you and your family. I wondered if I could just ask you a few quick questions about your visit?

Following Up on an Older Lead:

The reason I'm calling is, it's been some time since we last spoke and I wanted to follow up and see if I could ask you a few quick questions?

As you can see, each Reason Step is short and to the point.

Our goal is to accomplish our objective, not confuse the prospect in any way.

I have found that the more salespeople talk, the more guarded and confused prospects become. There is no need to over-explain anything, as the process is actually quite simple. Also notice that each step started with, *"The reason I'm calling is,"* and ended with gaining permission to ask questions.

You may also notice that I did not always state who I was with. In each case, it was assumed that I did that in Step Two, Disarming.

This leads us to one of the most important steps within the 5-Step Phone System: needs identification, which is part of what's called The Checkmate Question, Step Four. Realize that, prior to entering Step Four, you already have three to four yes responses in hand!

EXERCISE:

TAKE A MOMENT TO WORK THROUGH THE CONCEPTS WE HAVE BEEN WORKING WITH USING STEPS ONE THROUGH THREE.

You have been working with a family and they are in the decision phase. They are looking at two other communities and must make a decision by the end of the week (they have already toured your community). Using the Opening, Disarming, and Reason Steps, write out how you would make this call:

OPENING

_____

_____

_____

_____

DISARMING

_____

_____

_____

_____

THE REASON

Your objectives are to:

1. Uncover needs to create value

2. Relate and empathize with prospects

3. Listen

As discussed in the inquiry section of this training, you must ask questions to uncover needs and build value. This makes it clear that you care about what people feel and think. People really appreciate this, and can tell when you're sincerely interested. *Remember, people buy when they feel their needs are going to be met.* Just as you used the Inquiry Connection Sheets to identify enough needs to build value in regard to a visit, now you must use a Follow-up Connection Sheet to further identify needs in an effort to get a deposit. Worst case, you want to somehow move them forward in the sales process. Whether it's getting prospects to come back for an event, a second appointment with another decision maker, or even an appointment in their homes, something needs to happen.

GREAT NEWS!

You already learned how to do this. All you have to do is apply what you have learned to the follow-up process.

A FEW THINGS YOU SHOULD KNOW

Before introducing the Follow-up Connection Sheet, I would like to share a few statistics, courtesy of Total Census Solutions.

- ❑ 4 out of 5 inquiries will ultimately make a decision to move in somewhere

- ❑ 33% – within 3 months

- ❑ 33% – within 4 - 15 months

- ❑ 33% – within 16 - 39 months

- ❑ More than 60% of all leads make a decision after 3 months of consideration!

- ❑ 80% of all sales close after the 5th call

- ❑ Almost 50% of all salespeople give up after the 1st call, if unsuccessful

- ❑ 90% of all salespeople quit after the 4th call

Amazing, right? I love these kinds of numbers, because they help people understand the importance of what it is I am trying to teach. The bottom line? As I said before, "He who follows up, earns the sale!"

FOLLOW-UP PAYS OFF!

I had a great client that I had worked with on several occasions. The first time I spoke at their national convention, I sold over $85,000 in product, due to motivated attendees seeking to grow their businesses. The second time I spoke, I sold over $110,000 in product. I went on to speak there three more times. The last time, I called the client to see if they had a speaker need I could fill, and she said, "Yes!" The client went on to say that the reason they hired me over and over was because I was the only speaker/trainer they had worked with that followed up consistently over time, and it spoke volumes to them that I was teaching their sales field to do the very same thing. In essence, I was walking my talk!

In all, I sold over $300,000 for less than ten days of work! Don't get hung up on the sales...what I want you to get hung up on is what got me the sales—my follow-up skills.

Did I just get lucky? No! I called at the right time because I had asked them when they planned their conferences. I called again and again, and they hired me again and again. Imagine if I had not followed up at all; it would have cost me well over $200,000! If I had settled for the initial $85,000 in sales, I would have lost out on the balance.

Follow-up is critical to your overall success and in reality makes selling very easy to do.

THE BILD FOLLOW-UP SYSTEM

Before introducing you to the Follow-up Connection Sheet, I would like to challenge you to do two things with all new prospects who have had appointments with you. As mentioned throughout this book, I am a big believer in systems, particularly in a sales environment. Creating a system allows you to measure results and it creates good habits on the part of the sales professionals using them. Here are the first two things that must happen with all new leads, prior to using the Follow-up Connection Sheet.

1. Make a same day follow-up call.

2. Send a handwritten thank you note.

3. Call and use your Follow-up to a Visit Connection Sheet.

STEP #1: SAME DAY FOLLOW-UP CALL

It is important that you begin to follow up with people when they are interested. I realize this sounds like the most basic of statements, and it is. But the fact is, people are not doing it. As I mentioned, most sales counselors are either not following up at all, or waiting on average seven days before making their first follow-up call.

What people want to know is if you can be trusted. Are you really going to do what you say you are going to do after they move in? The best way to build their trust that you will deliver once they move is to earn their trust before they move. To do this, you must be diligent. Because of the aggressive competition in our industry, you can't wait even three days, let alone seven, to make a follow-up call!

I was on-site with a client and we went through leads that

had been pulled out of the database due to decisions to move elsewhere. What we found is that, while the sales counselor was "waiting" for the right amount of time to pass before making the follow-up call, the prospect was signing an agreement with their competitor. Stop thinking about what you would want and, instead, ponder what the prospect needs. In most cases, that is to move sooner rather than later. I personally believe that the individual with the strongest follow-up is the one who will, and should, earn the most sales in your local market.

All Bild Coaching students are trained to conduct same day follow-up calls. There is one rule to this call: you are not allowed to sell. Yes, you heard me right. Here is what I want you to do:

1. Call all prospects who had appointments with you on the same day they visited, ideally at the end of the day.

2. State that you are calling to thank them for taking the time to visit you.

3. Ask if any questions came up on the way home.

That's it!

Here is how your call might go:

Hi, is Mr. Clark in?

This is he...

Hi, Mr. Clark, it's Traci Bild calling...

Hi, Traci!

The reason I'm calling is, I just wanted to take a moment to thank you for coming in to visit our community today. I really enjoyed meeting you and also wanted to see if any questions came to mind after you left, as I know that's often the case.

Then, let the prospect talk. You will notice that I did Open the call but did not initiate the Disarming Step. As mentioned, the 5-Step System is flexible and since this call is going to be so short, I suggest you get right to the point.

When implementing the same day follow-up call, you will find that two things consistently occur:

1. People will be shocked that you called.

2. They will have lots of great questions.

Every student we have interviewed has said the same two things about the same day follow-up call. Prospects are pleasantly surprised they are calling, particularly on the same day of the visit. It demonstrates that you care and want to make sure they know you appreciate them coming to visit. Good, old-fashioned manners.

Secondly, our students love the fact that their prospects are asking lots of great questions, compared to the typical call a week later when they have none. It makes sense—don't we always think of everything we wanted to ask *after* we've left our appointments? Of course, and your prospects are no different. Call the same day and prompt them to ask questions, so you can provide great answers. Wait a week, and they won't only forget what questions they had, but exactly who you are!

Going forward, make same day follow-up calls a part of

your follow-up system. Start today! This means you r proactive and block thirty minutes out at the end of each day to make these calls to all visitors. If your executive director is willing to do these calls, it's even more powerful because they hold such influence.

STEP #2: THE HANDWRITTEN THANK YOU NOTE

Nothing is more powerful than the handwritten word. I'm not sure why, but every day I run to my mailbox in the hope of finding something personal. Come on, don't you do the same thing? For some reason, most of us love to check the mail. It's so popular here in our house that my husband and I literally run to the box to get there first (my reasoning is more so he doesn't scatter it all over the house). Yet rarely, if ever, is there anything other than bills and junk mail. Think about how good it feels on those rare occasions when a card or invite does come that is personalized to you. It's wonderful and so powerful that it keeps us coming back for more.

I find that, as a whole, our industry is really good at sending handwritten note cards. If you are currently doing this, great job! And be sure to keep it up within the boundaries of this system. If you are not, utilize our follow-up system and see what a difference they make. When considering your notes, I advise you to invest in stationery or note cards that reflect your personality. Corporately branded note cards simply are not personal. To build relationships, allow people to get to know you. My note cards are items that I find beautiful or that reflect my hobbies. I have cards with boats, travel, a soft pink color I find beautiful, and so on. Pick what you like and use this as an opportunity to express yourself.

When writing the note, keep it short and be sure to include something personal that reflects your prior conversation when together. It's important that people know the note card came from you and by mentioning something only you would know, it helps build trust and respect.

Lastly, do not use printed labels or a meter to stamp it. Handwrite the address and put a stamp on it. Personalized return labels are fine but use your name, not the community's.

STEP #3: THE FOLLOW-UP CONNECTION SHEET

Let's discuss what kind of questions are on the Follow-up Connection Sheet. Our end goal is to get the prospect to take some kind of action. Whether it's a second visit with an alternate decision maker, attending an upcoming event, or just having lunch, we want them to do something. Whenever making follow-up calls, think, "prospect advancement." The goal is to pick up the phone with purpose. Every contact with a prospective resident should be intentional.

I once had a personal coach who would say at the end of every coaching call, "Who are you going to be in the matter?" I would get frustrated because I didn't know what she meant. What does, "Who am I going to be in the matter?" even mean? And even when she explained it, I did not get it. Then, one day it clicked for me. What she was saying was, "What is your mental state going to be for the next week until we speak again?" Was I going to be focused, energized, and creative? Was I going to be open and receptive to the ideas that flowed my way? Was I going to be driven and determined? *Who I was going to be in the matter?* was designed to set my mind in a specific direction. So I'll ask, when you pick up the phone to call on the prospect who came in for a tour yesterday, "Who are you going to be in the matter?" Are you going to be long-winded, chatty, and friendly? Are you going to be determined to get a deposit? Focus on identifying enough needs that you can build value regarding the next action step, whatever you determine it to be—that's it!

As you saw with the stats I shared, most sales are not going to close in just 48 hours. It can be weeks, months, and for some, even years. What is important is that you know how to advance people in the process. When following up, you have to be intentional about what it is you are trying to accomplish. Otherwise, you will flounder and accomplish nothing.

STRATEGIC FOLLOW-UP

Prior to picking up the phone to call on a prospect, first think, *what is my end objective?*

Having a game plan makes closing much easier. Once you know what your end objective is, you can focus on asking the questions from the Follow-up to a Visit Connection Sheet. The goal is to build enough value, through needs identification, to get people to happily agree to the suggested next action step.

WARNING!

I have seen many of my coaching students assume that they know everything they need to know about a prospect once they have completed their initial Inquiry Connection Sheet and their personal visit. So instead of continuing the process of needs identification, they begin selling. Yet, the last thing they want to be perceived as is a salesperson. Isn't that ironic?

Here is my personal definition of sales: *The ability to identify needs and build value in regard to your product or service, in such a way that people will buy; the value built exceeds the pain felt in making a purchasing decision.*

It is critical that in the follow-up process you assume nothing. What you learned in the initial stage of the relationship may change as your prospect becomes more educated. For example, when Mrs. Smith called in, she might have said that what was most important to her was price and location. Yet after visiting your community, you may find on the follow-up call, when asking this question again, "Now that you have visited our community and learned a little more about retirement living, what's going to be most important to you?" She may say, "An active community with a strong social calendar is important. I've been to a total of four places and several of them had residents who just sat around in wheelchairs and some were actually sleeping on the lobby couches. I was horrified."

Imagine if you assumed price and location were still most important. You would have missed the boat and, of course, lost the sale entirely. Let's review the Follow-up Connection Sheet, on the next page, with a role-play scenario.

5-STEP PHONE PROCESS OVERVIEW FOR OUTBOUND CALLS

Connection Sheet
VISIT FOLLOW UP

Use Within 48 Hours
Of The On-Site Visit

DATE	PROSPECT NAME	PHONE	TEAM MEMBER

NOTES

*Same day call back and thank you card

Opening- "Hello may I speak with _____? Hi, _____ this is (your first and last name) calling."

Disarming- "If you recall, you visited us here at (name of community) on _____. Do you have a quick minute?

Reason- "The reason I'm calling is I wanted to thank you for your visit and wanted to ask you a few quick questions."

1. What was your overall impression of our community? _____

2. Now that you've visited our community, what have you found to be most important to you? _____

a. I can understand, so tell me how would you rate our ability to meet that need? _____

3. How do you feel our community compares to other options you are considering? _____

4. What is your deciding factor as far as a community you choose? _____

5. What other questions have come up as you've discussed this with your family? _____

6. Based on what we talked about today, on a scale of 1 to 10 with 10 being the highest how would you rate your level of interest in our community? _____

7. How ready are you to move to the next step? _____

So based on what you've told me it sounds like... (recap conversation)

The next step is _____

Offer option of two _____

TRAINING   COACHING   MYSTERY SHOPPING   MARKETING   SOCIAL MEDIA   CRM

BILD & CO.
INTEGRATED HEALTHCARE SOLUTIONS
800.640.0688
bildandco.com

CS 2.0-1-2015

133

EXERCISE:

Record yourself making a follow-up phone call on your own, without the Follow-up Connection Sheet. After listening to your side of the call, jot down your opinion of the call and the overall advancement of the prospect in the sales cycle:

_____

_____

_____

_____

Now record yourself making a follow-up call with the use of the Follow-up Connection Sheet. Note the difference in the overall conversation and prospect advancement:

_____

_____

_____

_____

If you did not see a considerable difference, repeat this exercise, because it was a fluke. You should have seen a tremendous difference in the overall quality of the conversation as well as a strengthening of your relationship with the prospect.

A TYPICAL FOLLOW-UP CALL

As coaches, we listen to thousands of mystery shops and recorded sales calls every year. Where performance is measured, it can be improved, and there is nothing more powerful than salespeople actually hearing themselves selling—it's compelling!

When following up, there are two statements I hear 98% of the time. Consider the examples below.

TYPICAL FOLLOW-UP STATEMENT #1: *Mrs. Smith, the reason I'm calling is, I just wanted to check in and see how you're doing...*

This conversation then typically proceeds to get entirely off track. It's not focused and so anything can happen. You might be stuck on the phone for an hour hearing about how her pet poodle had a severe kidney infection. Come on, you know this is true! Sadly, salespeople think that by listening for an hour they are building the relationship and gaining trust. The reality is, Mrs. Smith may really like you, but she is going to move to a community that meets her needs. It's that simple.

I once had a coaching student tell me this very thing happened to her. She had spent a large amount of time building a relationship with her client and talking to her on the phone, then one day she got a call and the prospect said, "I am so excited, and I just wanted to let you know that I made a decision to move to Pine Oaks," which was a direct competitor. She looked at my student as a friend—but not a solution.

You can build relationships and value regarding your community at the same time. As you notice on the Connection Sheets, the entire conversation is designed to be all about the prospects. They will love you! Have you ever met anyone who does not love to talk about themselves and what's important to them?

TYPICAL FOLLOW-UP STATEMENT #2: *Mrs. Smith, the reason I'm calling is, I wanted to touch base to see if you were still considering our community as an assisted living option?"*

The normal response to this popular question? No.

Think about it...would they really say yes even if they were still considering it? If they do, there is a risk you will begin to put the pressure on, which is something most people detest. Again, this is a dead-end question.

THE FOLLOW-UP TO A VISIT CONNECTION SHEET

Using the Follow-up Connection Sheet is a system that ensures you focus on the prospects' needs, at the current stage of their search. It forces you to focus and be intentional about understanding where they are mentally in their decision right now. It also allows you to know real timelines, level of interest in your community, and more. There will be no question in your mind as to where this prospect stands once you complete your Follow-up Connection Sheet.

THINK SYSTEMS!

Everything I have introduced you to so far has been built around a system. This is how you ensure results. Instead of just doing whatever you do or whatever you feel like at the present time, you are using a time-tested, proven system to get results.

1. Mismanaged call system

2. Inquiry system

3. Personal visit system

4. Follow-up system

Each of these systems is designed to fuel each aspect of the sales process.

GIVE PEOPLE CHOICES

Remember, before picking up the phone, determine your purpose. Why are you calling this person, and what is the end objective? Do not pick up the phone until you have this answer. Here are some reasons you may be calling back:

1. To ask for the deposit check

2. To invite to an event

3. To request an appointment with other decision makers

4. To extend an invitation for lunch, dinner, or a service such as a manicure or pedicure. The more you customize the service to a prospect's needs, the more successful you will be.

Whatever your end objective, try to close using an optional close. You should not go for any close without our two-step process in place:

1. Repeat needs back.

2. Utilize the Optional Close.

Let's say that I am calling to get the deposit on this call. Always start with Steps One and Two of the 5-Step Phone System to ensure you disarm the prospect and immediately engage him or her in conversation. Again, it's all about systems.

Hi, is Mrs. Smith in?

This is she...

Hi, Mrs. Smith, this is Traci Bild calling.

Hi, Traci, how are you?

I'm great, do you have a quick minute?

Sure...

The reason I'm calling, Mrs. Smith, is that I wanted to follow up with you in regard to our conversation here at The Meadows on Tuesday. When you were here, you had mentioned that you would be making a decision over the weekend and that a big part of that decision was the quality of the healthcare staff. You also mentioned that socialization was very important to you. I know that you were excited about the diverse activities we have here and the frequency of them, as well as our incredible staff. What I would like to do is invite you back in to fill out the paperwork and put down a deposit to hold the garden apartment that you love so much. Would it be easier for you to come here or would you prefer that I come visit you this time?

THEN PAUSE!

Notice that I repeated needs back and utilized the optional close. "No" is not an option. Of course, if she says, "I'm still not ready," you will respect that and continue to follow up.

The same format holds true if you are working to invite the prospect to an event. Always offer a choice of two events that would really appeal to the prospect. Odds are, one will work in her schedule and appeal to her.

Example: "We have two events I thought might appeal to you that are quickly coming up. One is our Italian Opera Night, and the other is the launch of our book club, since I know you love books. Which might you like to learn more about?"

PROSPECT ADVANCEMENT

When following up with prospects, you should always strategize the call prior to making it. Never call to just check in on people; have a game plan in mind to get them involved in your community, to better educate them about your services, or to bring value in some manner. The more people come to know and trust you, the more likely they will be to move in.

THE CLOSE

Because I don't like loose ends, I want to again complete the system and discuss the Checkmate Close Step. We have already discussed this, but it never hurts to review it again. It is closing, after all, which is something we can all use continued help with.

Checkmate Close

Your objectives are to:

1. Repeat needs back

2. Utilize the Optional Close

Human nature tells us that people take action based on their needs or motivations. This is the key to the close, showing that there is something in it for the prospect, not just a sale for you. Many times, inquirers don't know what it is they want until you begin to ask. For this reason, it's critical that when closing, you repeat the needs back to build value and validate their reason for calling.

After repeating the needs back, go right into a confident optional close. This means that you should give them a choice of two things they can pick from and that you want them to pick from...meaning NO is not one of the options. The most common close is, "So do you think you would like to come by sometime for a visit?" This makes me wonder, *I don't know, should I?* How can they be confident in their decision if you're not? You want to offer them a choice of today or tomorrow, morning or afternoon, and so on. Not the choice of yes or no!

EXAMPLE:

Mrs. Smith, based on what you've told me, it sounds like you have been caring for your husband for over five years. You are exhausted, both physically and mentally. Is that correct?

Yes.

You also mentioned that your husband is now in Stage Two of Alzheimer's and you are concerned because he is getting to be a bit more than you can handle. This is not to say you do not love him, because you do, tremendously. But the reality is, that you care for him enough to ensure he has the best of care and help in dealing with his Alzheimer's, is that correct?

Yes, it is.

Mrs. Smith, the next step at this point in time is for you to come in for a visit so you can meet our staff, sample our food, and interact with our residents. What would work better—tomorrow, or even this afternoon?

I can do this afternoon.

Great, would three or four o'clock work better for you?

Three would be great.

Will Mr. Smith be coming too, or just yourself?

Actually, it will be my daughter Mary and myself.

Okay. I look forward to meeting you, Mrs. Smith, and please, don't feel bad. You really are making the right choice by seeing what your options are. By the way, would you mind if I called

Mary to introduce myself and put her mind at ease, since she is coming with you? Of course I will follow up with you, but I would just like to make the most of your time here and a quick introduction allows visitors to be much more at ease when they arrive.

Okay, sure. Her number is 888.8823.

Thanks, Mrs. Smith. I'll see you today at 3:00.

THE OPTIONAL CLOSE

Notice that I gave Mrs. Smith options until there were none left. This makes it easy for people to say yes.

I have found closing to be one of the greatest challenges that people in sales face.

THE CLOSE SHOULD BE THE EASIEST PART OF THE SALE

If you implement the systems taught so far, you will never stress over the close again. Here is why: you will know in your gut that the value you have to offer your prospect far exceeds the pain of making a move. Yes, it is never easy for someone to sell a home he has lived in for 30 years or to suggest that a loved one live in a foreign environment rather than with a family member...these are stressful decisions, filled with guilt, regret, and more. However, if the value built regarding your community exceeds the pain felt, the decision will be effortless.

Whenever you are ready to close on anything, ask yourself, "Does the value built exceed the pain felt in making this choice?"

- ❏ Does the value built exceed the pain of writing a check for $125,000 for a community entrance fee?

- ❏ Does the value built exceed the pain of leaving a neighborhood one has lived in for 40 years?

- ❏ Does the value built exceed the fear of making a potentially wrong choice which one may regret for years to come?

It's your job to get people over the value threshold.

THE VALUE THRESHOLD: *The value built must exceed the pain felt.*

This is my definition of the value threshold. If you can do this, you can close anyone in due time. If someone says no when you request a deposit, it's not that they are being difficult; it's that you have not brought them over the value threshold. The only way to get a prospect over the value threshold is to ask more open-ended questions. The more you learn, the more value you can build. It's that simple. Why, oh why, do we make selling so hard?

Think of all the people you have had on your hot and warm lead list over the past six months, who did not buy. Did you know their core needs? What about their emotional needs? Could you have asked more questions and in turn, built more value? Once you learn to do this, your job as a sales professional will never be the same. You will love it more than ever, you will feel more professional and get more satisfaction, because you know you are making a difference in people's lives.

PRICE

The last thing I want to say about value is that once you learn to sell based on value built, price will no longer be an issue and you won't have to give concessions like many people do in this industry. Once your prospects know what's in it for them and they really see the value, they don't balk at the price. It's when they don't see the value that the price seems really, really high. Show people how to improve their overall quality of life and they will realize—that in itself is priceless.

EXAMPLE:

Many people balk at my fees. As a sales and customer service expert, I help companies drive revenue. Just as I've taught you, I find needs upon which to build value regarding my services. By the time I submit a proposal, I'm 95% certain I am going to close. I ensure that the value built exceeds the pain felt by my fee. I actually show clients what they are losing by not using my services. Suddenly my fee is a drop in the bucket compared to the value my client is getting. If someone does balk at the fee, then I know I've done a poor job identifying their needs and I have to go back and dig deeper.

KEY TO CLOSING

The most important thing I can say about closing is, do your homework up front. Take the time to ask lots of open-ended questions. Learn about your prospects' medical and emotional needs. The more you learn, the easier it will be to close.

LET'S BE REAL

You are not going to close every sale and people are going to object. The most important thing to remember is that when people are objecting, it's because they don't see the value in what you are trying to offer. Do not, in any way, try to overcome the objection. Instead, ask more questions in an attempt to better understand their needs. This is the fastest way to move the prospect forward in the sales process.

You must earn the sale. That means *work for it*. If the prospect is objecting, she does not see the value of what you are offering, it's as simple as that. All you have to do is uncover the driving need so you can, in turn, motivate the prospect to take action. The following are possible questions you can ask upon hearing an objection.

POSSIBLE QUESTIONS & ANSWERS

You know, I'm just not ready to make a decision. I'll call you back when I'm ready.

I understand, but while I have you on the phone, may I ask you one quick question?

Sure...

What initially prompted you to call in and learn about Riverview Gardens?

Well, I am just tired of taking care of this huge house all by myself, it's just gotten to be too much. What was once my pride and joy has become an embarrassment. Besides that, our neighborhood has gone down the toilet and I find myself hearing things all through the night. I just really wanted to explore other options for changing my situation.

By asking this Checkmate Question, you are able to determine what in particular prompted the prospect to call in and get her focused on her initial need to inquire. Using the example I just shared, you could then work to build greater value to this driving factor. A famous quote says, "Speak someone's language and they will follow you to the death." The only way you can learn your prospects' language is by asking questions and listening to what they have to say.

YOUR PRICE IS JUST TOO HIGH

If you hear prospects say this, realize that what they are really saying is that they do not see the value in paying the rate you have quoted in exchange for what they are getting. If you want to earn the sale, all you have to do is create value. This means that instead of overcoming their objection or basically arguing with them, you must instead ask a question that will uncover their specific needs in regard to a community.

YOU MIGHT SAY...

I understand, but while I have you on the phone, may I ask you one quick question?

Yes...

If price were not an issue, what would be most important to you about a community?

Well, I would say having things to do, such as outings, theater, socialization in general. I want to know that I am going to be active and not regret the decision I make.

You are now in a great position. You have knowledge that you can use to help the prospect make a connection between the service you can offer and the value it brings to her life. There is no need to talk anyone into anything, no need to get mad because she has not said yes, no need to attempt to overcome the objection. Just find the real need!

LET'S GET INTO THE MOST FRUSTRATING AND COMMON OBJECTIONS EXPERIENCED RIGHT NOW

I have to sell my home first.

I understand. Since we're on the phone, may I ask you one more quick question?

Sure...

If your home were to sell in just thirty days, what would be most important to you in regard to the community you would ultimately choose?

Oh gee, that would be great but trust me, my home is not going to sell in thirty days, sweetie!

I understand, but just for fun, let's say it did. What would be the deciding factors for you in regard to the community you would choose to call home? I heard you mention several times, socialization. Tell me more about that and what you're looking for in an ideal situation.

The goal is to focus your prospect on what it is he wants, not what he doesn't want. You and I can't do anything about the economy, stock market, or weather, which can be volatile. Since we can't control it, why focus on it? Your objective is to get the prospect interested enough that he will simply move to the next step in the sales process. If you can't do that, you don't have a prospect who's going to move any time soon. This prospect will continue to use the economy, market, or weather as an excuse, if not something else. It is important that when you hear objections, no matter what they are, you don't overcome them but instead provide solutions when you can and get right back to what it is your prospect wants. The value of what he wants must exceed the pain of what he doesn't want. When you can make that happen, you will earn a sale.

FINANCES

You must be comfortable discussing finances and utilizing the many financial tools your company has provided. I can say firsthand that the sales counselors we work with nationwide are not using financial worksheets to demonstrate what a prospect's financial picture will look like after moving to a community, compared to what it looks like pre-move. The only way to get comfortable doing this is to start. Think of it this way: you know more than they do. You are the expert who sells senior housing. My mother always told me, "Fake it 'til you make it!" It works, and the more you do it, the greater your confidence will become.

I want to make it clear that if your prospect owns a home, and needs to put it on the market, you will have difficulty moving forward without getting it on the market—so this has to be a top priority, if it is a barrier to closing. As a sales counselor, you want to direct prospects to a top rated realtor in your local market and get comps on their homes right away. A home comp will tell them what other homes similar to theirs is listed for, what they sold for, the length of time the home was on the market, and so on. This type of information will empower your prospect to make an educated decision based on facts versus thoughts or ideas. Other tools you might want to suggest to your prospects to help sell their homes are listed below.

- ❏ **Price:** Price is king, and those homes listed for the right price, and reflective of today's market, will move fastest. Although it's tempting to set a higher price and hope that the home will move, odds are it won't and the house will sit. And sit.

- ❏ **Show Appeal:** Encourage your prospects to move in *while* their home is on the market. Some providers are offering deferred rental payments, which allow their new residents to move in and pay when the home sells. The good aspect of this model is that moving the resident out of the home will allow it to show better because it's empty, can be repainted, re-carpeted, or more. Additionally, it can be traumatic for prospects to watch strangers walking through their homes.

- ❏ **Staging:** Should the prospect choose to stay in the home, offer to pay for a stager, who can come in and "stage" the home just as you do your models. The better the home shows, the faster it will sell.

❏ **Moving and Packing Services:** Partner with a moving and packing service who can handle the details of the move. For many seniors, just the thought of packing up an entire home and then moving can be overwhelming. This is why it's so important to dig down and understand what their fears and concerns are. It is to your advantage to offer to pay for this service, rather than reduce your monthly rent.

As part of the discovery process, you must identify what is standing between your prospects putting their homes on the market or leaving them to sit while they continue to research other options. The more resources and tools you can provide, the sooner they will take action.

WHAT ABOUT CONCESSIONS?

I want to address concessions. Far too many sales counselors are offering discounts and incentives up front, without any reason to do so. Our company conducts a large number of mystery shops each month. I often find that, without any prompting by the prospect, the sales counselor will say something like, "We are offering to waive our community fee and are giving $250 off the monthly rent for the first twelve months of living at our community."

But why offer concessions when it hasn't been identified that this is a barrier to closing? I believe that sales counselors do it in the hope of earning a quick, easy sale. I will say again, there are no easy sales. While you are offering a discount, it may be something as simple as an apartment closer to the dining room that would close the sale. Yet a sales counselor who

is focused on discounting is never going to get the sale.
not selling real estate; you are selling a better quality
Use concessions as a last resort and instead of just dropping
community fees and monthly rents (or entry fees), consider
offering a variety of tools or services that you can use at your
discretion:

- ❏ $1,000 toward a moving service

- ❏ $500 toward a packing company

- ❏ 90 days of free housekeeping services

- ❏ Carpet or cabinet upgrade

- ❏ A higher floor with a better view (if you are in a high-rise)
  for the same rate as a lower floor

These are just ideas but the point is, you don't need to give
away the store to entice people to buy now. If people see the
value, they will buy, case closed. If your competitors are giving away everything, including the kitchen sink, it is helpful
to have some incentives of your own that will make less of a
financial impact on your bottom line. People do like to feel
like they "got a deal." However, they will pay more if the value
justifies it. Never forget that.

MY COMPETITOR CHARGES WAY LESS THAN ME!

When coaching individual communities, we regularly hear,
"My competitors are $300 per month less than we are. How are
we supposed to compete?"

First, check your facts. On more than one occasion, we

have found these types of statements to be completely false. You have to focus on your community and the value it offers. Mercedes doesn't try to compete with Honda; they target two entirely different buyers. Have confidence in who you are, the fees you charge, and the value you deliver.

KNOW THY COMPETITORS

Shop your competitors once every six months, at minimum. It's important to know what services they are offering, rates they are charging, how they are positioning themselves in the market, and what specifically they are saying about you. Since the average prospect looks at four to six properties before making a move, the better you know them, the better you can compete. Here is the information you want to strive to obtain:

- ❏ Community fee

- ❏ Monthly rate ranges

- ❏ Move-in incentives

- ❏ Services provided

- ❏ Transportation options

- ❏ Entry fee packages and healthcare plans

- ❏ Current number of residents (if you can get it)

- ❏ How they are selling (compared to you)

This basic information will better equip you to differentiate your community and make it stand out. This also will help you to clarify any misguided information you may have in regard to what the competitors are offering. Knowledge is power!

MORE ON CLOSING

I have outlined below a series of Checkmate Questions and Optional Closes you can ask of prospective residents you are trying to close and who are objecting.

The closing process always begins with recapping to build value:

"So, based on what you told me it sounds like... (Repeat needs—this is when you need to talk. The more needs you have identified, the greater the value you will build)," then present the Optional Close:

"The next step is _____ (coming in for a visit, choosing an apartment, financial review, more Q and A, etc.). What might work best for you, _____ or _____ ? (offer two options)

If the prospect chooses one of your options, go from there. If the prospect does not choose one, but instead gives an objection (*I want to think about it, we want to go home and discuss it further, we have to talk to Mom, we need more time, we want to wait until the spring, summer, winter, fall, etc.*), you then move to a Checkmate Question, which always begins with:

"I completely understand. Do you mind if I ask you a quick question?"

or

"Before you go, can I ask you one more quick question?"

CHECKMATE CLOSE QUESTIONS TO CHOOSE FROM:

1. *You and I have been speaking for (quite some time, a month, a year, one week, etc.) and I was wondering, what was it that made you call in initially? Start your search? Prompted your first phone call? Made you decide to walk in that first day?*

2. *In looking to the future, what do you think will be the #1 deciding factor in a community you will choose for (you, your mom, etc.)?*

3. *I know you are not ready to make a decision for another (six months/ one year), but can I ask, "What was it that made you decide to begin your search today?"*

4. *You mentioned you are just starting your search and are looking to make a move in 1-2 years. Can I ask, "What in particular made you decide to call me today?"*

5. *On a scale of 1-10, with 10 being the highest, where would you say you are on the scale as far as making a decision to move to our community? What is your level of interest in making a move to our community over the others you have visited? If not a 10: What could we do to help make that a 10?*

6. *I sense some hesitation (resistance or tension) in moving to the next step in this decision-making process. Could I ask what might be causing this hesitation (resistance or tension)?*

7. *We've been talking for quite some time now (be specific).*

Recap to build value and then ask, "What will it take to help you make a decision to set a move-in date today?"

8. *Can I ask, now that you've visited our community and several others, what is the most important factor in regard to a community's amenities and services that will help you ultimately choose?*

9. *What in particular is holding you back from making a decision today?*

10. *If I can ask you to imagine your mother (paint mental picture of mom living in your community, i.e., safe, laughing with friends, eating regularly and having fun during meals, getting the medications she needs at the appropriate times, enjoying the garden/outdoors on her daily walk, etc.), how might that make you feel? How might it make you feel to truly enjoy being her daughter again and seeing her embrace a new quality of life?*

SPECIFIC OBJECTIONS & CHECKMATE QUESTIONS TO ASK:

11. *"I'm just not ready."* Ask: *What, in particular, do you mean when you say that you are not ready? Or, what will the day look like to you when you feel that you will be ready?*

12. *"I need to talk to my_____(son, daughter, husband, wife, family member) first."* Ask: *When will you be talking to_____ next? How do you think _____ will feel? Would it be helpful to conduct a three-way conference call with you, _____, and myself?*

13. *"I want to spend one more _____ (Christmas, Holiday, birthday, family reunion, etc.) in my home"* *Utilize the "Feel, Felt, Found technique." For example, I completely understand how you feel, and quite honestly, a lot of our residents felt the same way that you do right now. What they have found is that*

    <u>   </u>

    <u>   </u> .

14. *"I just don't think that I can afford it." Complete a cost comparison and determine if they may qualify for Veterans Benefits or have Long Term Care Insurance, a Life Insurance Settlement, or even a financial planner they work with...or perhaps you can recommend one to them.*

15. *"I need to wait until after my surgery for _____."* *Discuss post-surgical care options through third parties (for example, Physical Therapy, Occupational Therapy, Wound Care, etc.).*

IMPORTANT SUCCESS TIPS

❏ Be confident in what you are offering the prospect. People want to buy from those who are passionate about what they do. Even if you are new, make a recommendation and stand behind it with 100% confidence.

❏ Put the prospect's mind at ease by reassuring him that he is making the right decision. Many times you will hear prospects pause and you will see hints of insecurity come through in regard to their decision to inquire about your services. When noticing this, speak up. You might say, "Joe, you are doing the right thing by learning about the various options available to your father." Or, "Ann, you are going to see a dramatic improvement in the overall quality of your relationship with your mom once she makes a move into a community such as ours. You will once again be mother and daughter, versus mother and caretaker, and that will ease both of your minds."

❏ Prospects are people, just like you. Do not be intimidated by them. The more you relate on a personable yet professional level, the more successful you will be. People like to do business with those they are comfortable with.

❏ You know more than they do. If you are new and insecure about the knowledge you possess in regard to your services, remember that you still know more than they do. Do your best and work to learn as you go, the best that you can.

❑ The Checkmate Question allows you to take the focus off of what is causing the prospect to object and instead puts it on the need, which is what matters most.

❑ To close any kind of sale, you must match the prospect's need to a solution, it's that easy.

❑ By nature, you will want to overcome the prospect's objection. Using this questioning strategy will take discipline and a determination to really want to help the prospect find a solution.

You might have had different questions than those I picked to use in these examples. When looking at your questions, if they are open-ended and designed to uncover the prospect's needs, then your answers were correct.

When you identify a prospect's core need, you will automatically know that you are going to close, and will feel it! The reason you will know is because it makes sense—not just to you, but to the customer too.

> *"Develop confidence in yourself and act as*
> *if you have it until you do."*
> —Barbara Krouse

> *"Serve the customer. Serve the customer.*
> *Serve the customer."*
> —Bernard Marcus

IMPORTANT SUCCESS TIPS REGARDING THE 5-STEP PHONE SYSTEM

❑ When you put a process in place that allows you to follow a system instead of just "winging it" when talking with prospects, you will have much more success.

❑ By having a system, you can ensure that you, not the prospect, are in control of the call. In sales, typically the prospect is in charge and determines where the call will go. Not true with this system.

❑ Because you know what you are going to say before saying it, you can easily predict what the prospect is going to say. Fear of the phone comes from the unknown. In this system, there is no unknown, and therefore nothing to be afraid of.

❑ People who learn to overcome their call reluctance and fear of the telephone call will have less stress and more success.

❑ Obtaining three yes responses will put prospects in a positive state of mind and make them more willing to open up to you.

❑ 85% of sales success stems from relationships formed. Using the 5-Step Phone System ensures that you are connecting with the prospect and forming an immediate relationship.

❑ Identifying yourself by both first and last name at the beginning of the call instead of by your company's name will keep prospects from becoming guarded or armed.

❏   If prospects feel threatened, they will work to get you off the phone. If they feel comfortable, they will not mind talking openly with you.

❏   Never show and tell; instead, find needs to sell—always!

MESSAGES

It's amazing what a popular question this is: *do I leave a message?*

If you have been in sales before, then you know that if you leave a message, prospects will not call you back. Sure, they may once in a blue moon, but in reality they just don't. I have found that even if the prospect listens to your message and wants to speak with you, they are not going to step out of their comfort zones to pick up the phone and call you back. It sounds silly, but it's just too much work.

When making calls, whether a first time contact or a follow-up call, I suggest the following rule of thumb:

When attempting to reach prospects, call three different times, actually trying to reach them. If, on the fourth attempt no one is there, go ahead and leave a message. Doing this will allow you to try different time frames in an effort to actually "catch" them at some point during the day or week. There is no law that says you must leave a message and if you do, they will then watch the caller ID from that point forward to avoid you. When leaving a message, follow the 5 Steps. This will keep your message focused and ensure that you do not ramble. Here is an example:

> *Hi Rhonda, this is Traci Bild calling. If you recall, you came in and toured with me here at Sterling Place. The reason I'm calling is, I wanted to thank you so much for coming in and wanted to ask you just a few quick questions about your visit. If you get a minute, I would like to briefly speak with you. You can reach me at 887.1234 and my extension is 456. Again, my name is Traci Bild and my number is 887.1234, extension 456. Thanks, Rhonda, and I hope to talk with you soon.*

IMPORTANT SUCCESS TIPS

❏ State both your name and number twice, in case the person is writing it down.

❏ Speak slowly when giving your number. Many people actually speed this part of the call up, and prospects couldn't call back if they wanted to.

❏ If you have an unusual name, spell it for the prospect in case she is writing it down.

❏ Be enthusiastic so that he will want to call you back.

REMEMBER, YOU CAN'T CLOSE A SALE UNLESS YOU SPEAK WITH THE PROSPECT. DON'T JUST LEAVE MESSAGES; ACTUALLY WORK TO CONNECT WITH THE PROSPECT AND CREATE THE SALE.

YOUR FIRST WEEK OF FOLLOW-UP WITH ALL NEW PROSPECTS

I have outlined what happens the first week of a prospect's appointment:

1. Make your same day follow-up thank you call.

2. Send a handwritten thank you note.

3. Within 48 hours of the visit, utilize your Follow-up to a Visit Connection Sheet.

You may be a bit worried about such aggressive follow-up when perhaps you are not doing anywhere near this right now. This may be why you are not moving ten plus apartments per month (unless you are full). You *can* do this! Keep in mind that the same day follow-up call is a simple thank you and to ask if there are any questions. The Follow-up to a Visit Connection Sheet that is used 48 hours later is designed to help you figure out where the prospect is in the process. So you are comfortable, you might say something like this:

> *Mrs. Smith, I know we just spoke a few days ago, but I did want to follow up with you and ask a few quick questions while our community is fresh in your mind. Do you mind if I ask you a few questions?*

You are addressing the fact that you did speak to her following the visit, that is, if you were able to reach her and not leave a message, and the goal of that call was to just check in. The goal of today's call is to learn what her experience was with your community and how perhaps it compares to some of the other options she is considering.

WOW, WOW, WOW!

Imagine...your prospect has visited three to four properties and no one has followed up with her at all—nada. Yet in the first week, she had a polite thank you call that made her feel important, a beautiful note showed up in her mailbox, and you had the courtesy to call her and take the time to ask what she felt about the community, what her concerns were, what discoveries she made, and more. You, not your competitors, have made her feel valued and important. That is how you forge relationships and build value in regard to your community.

WHAT IF THE PROPSECT DOES NOT SCHEDULE A VISIT?

If a prospect phones in but does not agree to schedule a visit, you still want to send a thank you note. For some readers this will seem like a waste of time. It's important to remember that this is a process. Your first goal is to build a strong connection with callers. Imagine how surprised your prospect will be, after calling four to five (or more) communities to gather information, to get a thank you note in the mail from you. When it comes time to schedule visits, who do you think will be at the top of the list, and memorable? YOU!

Once the brochure is sent, I suggest following up weekly with phone calls and offer to provide other valuable resources that will help make the search easier. Each call will focus on asking great open-ended questions to learn about your prospect and end with the two-step close as outlined in this book. Your top priority is to get people on-site to experience your community firsthand.

WEEK #2 FOLLOW-UP

I specifically want to focus on the first 30 days of follow-up because I feel it's what you can handle. Odds are, the systems you are reading about appear to be very basic. Yet as you begin to implement them you are going to find that they are indeed challenging. Your first follow-up goal will be to master the thirty-day system I outline in this chapter. Once you are consistently implementing, you will move on to month two, three, four, and so on.

In week two, you want to continue to be diligent in your follow-up. Always remember to follow up early in the sales process with prospects—while they are interested. Just as in week one, week two will focus on creating value. Here is what I would like for you to do in your second week of follow-up for each prospect you work with (qualified):

1. Send a timely article.

2. Follow up with a phone call and utilize your Follow-up to a Visit Connection Sheet #2.

SEND A TIMELY ARTICLE

Choose two different articles that will appeal to your prospects. A CCRC may provide an article on entry fees, while a Memory Care community may select one that deals with the guilt adult children face when moving their loved ones to a Memory Care community. Your selection should be something that is relevant to their decision to call you, informative, and written by a respected third party.

To build trust, you must earn it. Taking the time to follow up three times in the first week of a prospect's visit and then twice in the second week will make a tremendous impact. In week one, your goal is to learn as much as possible about your prospects. Using the Inquiry Connection Sheet, the Visit Planning Sheet, and the Follow-up to a Visit Connection Sheet will help you make sure this happens. Week two provides an opportunity to further connect and build more trust. By sending something that is helpful to your prospect, yet not specifically promoting your community, it proves that you care and want to help. Imagine how your prospects will feel when they receive a great article that addresses the very challenges they are dealing with!

HERE ARE ARTICLE SAMPLES:

- ❏ Funding Senior Housing
- ❏ Assisted Living: Affordable Care Choice
- ❏ What Is Assisted Living?
- ❏ Picking the Right New Home

- ❏ A Family Crisis

- ❏ Blue Mood

- ❏ Senior Housing: How to Live Independently

- ❏ Helping Your Loved Ones Adjust

- ❏ Tips on Talking with Aging Parents

- ❏ The New Face of Independent Living

Do any of these look interesting to you? Odds are, you're wanting to get your hands on them right now! What's important is that you understand that each article speaks to someone who is dealing with a senior housing issue. The more they understand about the services we provide, the experiences others have had who have gone through the same thing, and so on, the sooner they will make their decisions. In short, this is an incredible opportunity to provide value, early on in the sales process.

I suggest that you select several articles that you feel will make the most impact. Put them in a file and select which one would be the best fit for prospects as you follow up in week two. If you manage an organization, consider selecting a variety of articles for your sales counselors. It is also important to update your article selection at least quarterly.

When sending your article, consider putting a sticky note on the folded article that says, "Hi, Janet, this is something I thought you might find helpful!" You might even have hand-written sticky notes pre-made that say, "Thought you might find this helpful, Traci." Do not include a cover letter, as they are too formal. Our goal is to personalize each step of the sales process.

The second follow-up step in week two is to make another phone call. Remember that those who sell ten or more apartments per month have, use, and trust their sales systems. I know this seems like a lot, but you will see the payoff in your increasing numbers.

THE FOLLOW-UP TO A VISIT CONNECTION SHEET #2

You will use the Follow-up to a Visit Connection Sheet #2 for this call (see the sample on the following page). The goal of the call is to set a follow-up appointment with your prospect. The good news is, you have already learned how to use the various Connection Sheets and understand the 5-Step Phone System. Now it's just a matter of asking a different series of questions that will make an impact at this particular stage of the sales process.

When using this tool, you will first attempt to schedule an appointment. If the prospect says "no" to your offer, you will flip the page over and ask more questions in an attempt to build value. When people decline your offers, in short, it means there is nothing in it for them. That means you have more work to do. Upon asking the questions as outlined on the next page and listening to your prospect's responses, you will then attempt to schedule an appointment one more time. This is assuming you were able to identify more needs and, in turn, create more value. You won't schedule everyone, so don't get discouraged if you are not successful. This system will help you to hit a 50% contact to appointment conversion ratio, at minimum.

WHAT IS YOUR CALL TO ACTION?

When making follow-up calls in week two, try to think out of the box. What events or activities are going on that your prospect might enjoy? Is there a trip that might be enticing, an educational seminar, or a garden club project? The more customized the offer to come and experience the community further, the more likely you will get a yes to your request.

Complete Follow-up Step 4 Connection Sheet™ #2

Date: _____   Your Name: _____

Prospect Name: _____   Phone: _____

WEEK #2 FOLLOWING THE ON-SITE VISIT

Follow Up STEP 1: Did you or your Admin do the SAME DAY thank you call back? ☐ Y ☐ N
Follow Up STEP 2: Did you send a thank you note the day of or after your visit? ☐ Y ☐ N
Follow Up STEP 3: Did you complete your Follow Up to a Visit Connection Sheet in Week 1? ☐ Y ☐ N

Hi _____, this is _____ (1st & last name) calling... **PAUSE**

DISARM
a. (If they **do not** recognize you by name) *If you recall (you visited our community on Monday, we spoke yesterday afternoon, etc.) _____* **PAUSE**

b. (If they **do** recognize you by name) *Do you have a quick minute?*

The Reason *I'm calling is it's been _____ (a week or so) since we last spoke and I was wondering if I could ask you a few quick questions?*

Did you receive the _____ (article, testimonial, information) I sent you a few days ago?

What did you find most helpful? (Drill down- Great, tell me a little more about that?)

Have you been able to (visit other communities in our area, discuss with your family, etc) since our last conversation (EXPLORE what if yes)?

EVENT OPTIONS

(EACH month pick two fun & interesting events / services to showcase to your prospects that they can attend. Make them ENTICING!)

Close: ***Based on what you have told me.....(repeat needs/wants) The next step would be to come experience our community first hand. There are a couple of things going on that I thought might be of interest to you. The first is _____ & the second is _____. Which would you like to learn more about?***

IF THEY SAY NO, UTILIZE THE CLOSING CONNECTION SHEET (LIME)

© Bild & Co. ★ www.TraciBild.com ★ 800.640.0688 ★ **February 2013** ★ Color Code: Yellow

IF PROSPECTS SAY NO THANKS, GO TO ADDITIONAL QUESTIONS!

I understand. While I have you on the phone may I ask you a couple of QUICK questions?

As you've continued to do more research into AL/IL what stands out as most important to you in regard to choosing a community? (Relate to them)

May I ask how the communities you've visited compare to what you had in mind when you began your search? (Relate)

What will have to happen in order for you to consider making a move to our Community and truly experiencing all of the benefits we have to offer?

Checkmate Close: Based on what you told me, it sounds like...(Recap) Again, I feel it would be really beneficial if you could come back in and (let me introduce you to a few residents, show you our floor plans again, etc.) now that you know what to expect; it can be overwhelming for people the first time around. Would you by chance be available tomorrow or would this afternoon perhaps work for you? (Optional Close)

WEEK #3 FOLLOW-UP

Odds are, your prospect is engaged and responding to your personalized follow-up effort. If not, you need to red flag the lead and schedule a home visit in week three. Home visits are incredibly beneficial and will help you to better understand what's happening. The home visit will trump the suggestions I make here as to what should happen in week three.

I imagine if you are a CCRC or entry fee community of any kind, you're thinking, "Not me, I am not doing a home visit!" That is exactly why you should. Your competitors would not even consider it. Whether a prospect is in need of Independent or Assisted Living, they ALL like to feel important. Dropping by with three days of freshly prepared meals that simply need to be put in the oven would make a strong impact on even the toughest of leads. Again, this is a great strategy for hot leads that are beginning to turn warm or cold.

For those leads that are engaging, here is what I would like for you to do in your third week of follow-up:

1. Mail a resident or family testimonial.

2. Make a follow-up phone call and invite him/her to an event.

MAIL A RESIDENT OR FAMILY TESTIMONIAL

People are skeptical, particularly when it comes to senior housing. While they may not believe what you tell them, they will believe what your residents or their family members say. Third party endorsements are incredibly powerful. Whenever someone gives you a great compliment say, "Can I get a quote from you?" Write down the quote and send it to them for approval. You can then use these in ads, collateral material, or on your website.

Select your best testimonial and utilize it in week number three, just as we sent an article in week two. If you don't have any letters, create a contest that encourages your residents to write them. You will be stunned at the impact these letters can make. This step, combined with those taken so far, will continue to build value in regard to your community and move you one step closer to a move-in.

FOLLOW-UP PHONE CALL

In week three, make another follow-up call. There is no Connection Sheet to use. Simply utilize the 5-Step Phone System and determine what your Reason Step for calling will be. Every call should have an end objective. You must know what it is you are going to close on. Always strive to move the prospects forward in the sales process. The more they experience your community, the easier a move will be.

WEEK #4 FOLLOW-UP

Finally, week number four. This week, I would like for you to address finances. Either e-mail or mail the financial worksheet I have provided, or one of your own. You want to encourage people to review the financial probability of making a move to your community if they have not yet done so. People tend to make assumptions, and those will oftentimes kill your sale. Instead of looking at the facts, people assume it will cost more to make a move. Allow prospects to review the facts and accurately understand what the financial difference will be, whether negative or positive, upon making a move.

During this same week, make another follow-up call. Keep in mind that you won't always reach your prospects. You will speak with some and leave messages with others. You will also strive to set the agreed upon next steps in place with each prospect. Clearly those steps would precede these. However, if someone says, "I'm not moving for a year," you do want to continue with this plan. Be sure to state that you understand and that you want to be a resource for them. So long as you are not acting like a salesperson but are, instead, focused on finding needs and building value, people will be fine with you following up. Always defer to their requests on follow-up timing to show respect.

IMAGINE THE DIFFERENCE

Imagine the difference in sales if you were to follow this four-week plan with each and every lead. Keep in mind that it will require organization, a good contact management system, and discipline on your part. In a decade of helping thousands of sales counselors work with leads, I can tell you with confidence that this plan will help you get the move-ins needed to fill your community. Compare what I have outlined to what you are doing now. If you manage an organization, think about what this could do for your bottom line. You and I both know that the follow-up simply is not happening. We can't expect people to move if we don't actively get them excited to do so! This system can be the greatest differentiating factor in the sales process between you and your competitors.

HE WHO FOLLOWS UP WILL EARN THE SALE.

FINANCIAL WORKSHEET

AMOUNT NEEDED TO MEET NEEDS: $_____ /
Mo. Annual Increase: _____

% CURRENT EXPENSES	$ AMOUNT
Mortgage / Rent	$ _____
Home Insurance	$ _____
Taxes	$ _____
Utilities	$ _____
Phone	$ _____
Water	$ _____
Transportation	$ _____
Current Care Expenses	$ _____
Cable	$ _____
Total Mo. Expenses	$ _____

CURRENT MO. INCOME	$ AMOUNT	PROJECTED END DATE
Pension	$ _____	/ /
Social Security	$ _____	/ /
Investment Income	$ _____	/ /
Rental Income	$ _____	/ /
Other	$ _____	/ /

Total Mo. Income $ _____

Total Mo. Expenses .... $ _____

Current Net Difference .... $ _____

Total Community Fees Mo. .... $ _____

Future Net Difference.............. $_____

Which option appeals most so far?

_____ Our Community

_____ Staying Put

ASSETS	$ AMOUNT
Value of Home	$ _____
Savings	$ _____
Investments	$ _____
Investment Properties	$ _____
LTC Policy	$ _____

OTHER OPTIONS	$ AMOUNT
Family Contributions	$ _____

CHAPTER 6

THE 100% OCCUPANCY SYSTEM

The "magic number" is a term our team uses to assess how many apartments are needing to be filled. You will notice I did not say to hit budget, but instead, to fill. If you have a property with 150 apartments, your objective should be to fill all 150 apartments, not just 130.

To fill, you must first understand what stands in the way, and then close the gap. First, what is your magic number? How many open apartments do you have right now? How long will it take, based on your average monthly move-ins, to fill? I always challenge our coaching students to double their monthly move-ins as quickly as they can. To accomplish this task, you have two choices: you can work smart or hard.

WORK SMART

A senior housing sales counselor who works smart does the following:

- ❏ Knows occupancy and the magic number to fill at all times.

- ❏ Works with the back-up team to consistently ensure all leads are being captured and stellar service is provided.

❏ Utilizes 90% or more of the Inquiry Connection Sheet on all phone and walk-in inquiries.

❏ Is more interested in understanding the needs of the prospect than sharing how amazing his community is.

❏ Is an active listener.

❏ Drills down and seeks to learn details about her prospect.

❏ Actively closes each call or visit by recapping the conversation and utilizing an optional close.

❏ Collects two phone numbers and an e-mail (in total, prior to getting off the phone) as a top priority so follow-up is effective.

❏ Has a 50%+ inquiry to appointment conversion when selling CCRC or IL, and 75%+ when selling Assisted Living, Memory Care, or SNF products.

❏ Completes a Visit Planning Sheet on all pre-scheduled appointments and uses a full Inquiry Connection Sheet on walk-ins.

❏ Does not overcome objections but instead focuses prospects on what it is they want.

❏ Asks for the check (when appropriate) and always schedules a next action step so the prospect knows what to expect.

❏ Follows up aggressively and early in the sales process so he or she doesn't have to work so hard on the back end.

❏ Makes between 20-30 follow-up calls per day.

❏ Utilizes the Bild 5-Step Phone System to increase phone out to appointment conversions.

❏ Has a visit to move-in conversion of 20%+ for CCRC, 35%+ for Independent Living, 50%+ for Assisted Living and 75%+ for Skilled Nursing Center.

❏ Has a zero lost revenue day mindset and understands that the community is at its success peak when full.

That's a lot to take in, wow! Still think these systems are elementary? To get results, you don't have to have a program that is difficult to understand and completely "new." You need a system that can be quickly implemented and that is measurable.

METRICS

The final piece of the puzzle that pulls everything else together is metrics. What's measured can be improved, and numbers allow you to quickly identify gaps you can quickly close with the systems in this book. When working with communities, we look at the data. I have found that some reports our clients use are so cumbersome that their own people won't even look at them. It's important to review the following metrics weekly.

1. Inquiries: Measures if, indeed, you have traffic

2. Telephone Inquiry to Appointment Conversion: Answers the question, "Are you converting inquiries into on-site visits?"

3. Total Visit to Move-in Conversion: Determines your ability to find needs, build value, and move prospects to residents.

4. Monthly Move-ins: Ensures you are netting enough move-ins to offset move-outs for a positive net growth.

5. Move-outs: Keeps the outs front and center at all times to create urgency in growing move-in numbers, and also to collaborate with operations on any residents who move due to dissatisfaction.

6. Occupancy Percentage: Current units occupied, which should consistently trend up until you reach 93-94%, drive rents due to the pricing power occupancy provides, and ultimately move to 100% occupancy, for zero lost revenue days.

NUMBERS DON'T LIE

Conversion Matrix	Jan 13	Feb-1	Mar 13	Apr-1	May 13	Jun 13	Jul 13	Aug 13	Sep 13	Oct 13	Nov 13	Dec 13	YTD
Total Inquiries	25	32	43	29	32	37	36	-	-	-	-	-	177
Total Inquiries Contacted	16	25	25	20	21	29	22						158
Total Personal Visits Booked from Calls	4	7	8	7	10	15	12						63
% Conversion (Visit Ratio)	25.0%	28.0%	32.0%	35.0%	47.6%	51.7%	54.5%	0.0%	0.0%	0.0%	0.0%	0.0%	39.9%
Total First Personal Visits, Including Walk-Ins	8	12	13	13	20	22	28						116
Total Deposits Received from first visits	-	1	1	-	2	3	2						9
% Conversion (First Visit Close Ratio)	0.0%	2.0%	7.7%	0.0%	10.0%	13.6%	7.1%	0.0%	0.0%	0.0%	0.0%	0.0%	7.8%
Total Personal Visits, including Re-Visits, Walk-Ins	12	14	13	18	16	19	22						114
Total Deposits for Month	2	3	4	5	6	8	9						37
% Conversion (Deposit Ratio)	16.7%	21.4%	30.8%	27.8%	37.5%	42.1%	40.9%	0.0%	0.0%	0.0%	0.0%	0.0%	32.5%
Total Personal Visits, including Re-Visits, Walk-Ins	12	14	13	18	16	19	22						114

Total Move-ins, including respites	3	3	5	4	5	6	8						34
% Conversion (Closing Ratio)	25.0%	21.4%	38.5%	22.2%	31.3%	31.6%	36.4%	0.0%	0.0%	0.0%	0.0%	0.0%	29.8%
Total Prospect Follow-Up Calls (made or received)	49	62	59	60	65	68	70						433
Appointments Scheduled from Follow-Up Calls	8	15	12	12	15	20	21						103
% Conversion (Lead Base to Appointment Ratio)	16.3%	24.2%	20.3%	20.0%	23.1%	29.4%	30.0%	0.0%	0.0%	0.0%	0.0%	0.0%	23.8%
Total Move-ins	3	3	5	4	5	6	8						34
Total Move-outs	4	2	3	2	4	5	3						23
Month End Occupancy %	92.8%	92.0%	93.0%	93.5%	94.0%	94.0%	95.0%						

In looking at the numbers in the conversion matrix shown above, you can see that this community has consistent traffic, meaning there is indeed an interest in what they are offering. Year to date, the inquiry to appointment conversion is 39.9%. The average Assisted Living community converts 40% of all inquiries into an on-site visit. If they were to increase their conversion to 60%, our minimum benchmark, with the use of proven systems, that would in effect add another 32 on-site visits year to date. Getting more people in the door is the #1 factor proven to drive occupancy. It pays to work smart!

The total visit to move-in conversion from January to June was just 29.8%. Industry-wide, 22% of all Assisted Living tours move in. While above average, if this community were to grow their visit to move-in to just 35%, they would have seen an additional six move-ins, and that's based on just 39% of inquiries converting to tours. While it may not seem like a lot, six additional move-ins is an increase of $288,000 in annual revenue, at minimum.

COMMUNITY TARGET FOCUS: CLOSING SKILLS

For this community (an actual client of ours in the Midwest), the focus should be to grow the inquiry to tour to a minimum of 60% and total visits to move-in to a minimum of 50%. These small gains yield big results. Once these benchmarks are hit, the next goal is a 75% inquiry to tour and a 50% total tour to move-in. It's a game of inches, and every gain counts!

I remember when I first met with this one client, they were considering using me but I was competing with three other firms. Prior to my visit, I had three telephone mystery shops done and an on-site shop. This was part of my due diligence to better understand what the true challenges were at this location. Keep in mind that I didn't know at first if I was going to get the contract, yet I did my homework, invested my own money in conducting mystery shops, and prepared a detailed review of exactly what their problem was. In short, I do exactly what I am telling you to do: prepare. By the time I flew in, I knew I would get the contract because I was prepared and had 100% confidence I could change the financial picture of this community. This is how you should feel as you conduct your appointments. You should have the confidence that, without a doubt, you can close because you prepared and can deliver on the prospect's identified needs.

When meeting with my client, I played recordings of the mystery shops and reviewed the on-site shop. They were absolutely shocked and, I believe, impressed that I came so prepared. While I was able to clearly identify where the gap between their current occupancy and 100% was, closing both on the phone and in person, the other firms were telling them they needed to do more marketing. This meant not only hiring a consulting firm to help with the community, but also dumping a lot of money into marketing. I couldn't believe my ears, because it was clear they had enough traffic, they just were not closing at the conversion rates they should have been reaching.

You won't believe how many people go this route. They believe advertising will solve all their problems. You have to pay close attention to your metrics so you know where to put your efforts. Once I got the contract for this new client, we began working immediately on closing skills. In just two short months of working together, we began to see substantial results. The same can hold true for you. Utilize metrics and see what's really happening, then apply one or more of the many systems outlined in this book to bring change.

CHAPTER 7
FINAL THOUGHTS

IN CLOSING

I have so much information in my head, I could write forever. While writing this book, I kept going back and adding more but realized it's not how much information one has, but what he or she chooses to do with it. Much of my success in life comes from my ability to follow through. When I start a project, I finish it (I didn't say it was easy). I challenge you to pick two systems from this book and make a commitment to implement them. Follow through and see the payoff in sales and revenue.

Although we are in the business of selling senior housing, we are really about caring for people. You have the opportunity to make a positive impact on people in the years when they feel most vulnerable. The seniors you are working with no longer work, and most are living off the income they generated during their careers. While someone may have a high net worth, it doesn't mean they are not frightened at the thought of losing it or spending it frivolously.

While we are asking for the seniors we work with to spend their money with us, we are also asking them to make incredibly difficult decisions, such as selling their homes. We can simply say, "It's time to put your home on the market." However, for that prospect you are working with, her home is her story, where all her memories were created, and saying goodbye is like closing the fifteenth chapter of a sixteen-chapter book. She feels finality, like the end is more near than ever. Yes, we are asking her to ponder these very thoughts, along with the reality that, once a decision is made, she can never go "home" again because that home will be gone, with a new family starting their life story in what was once her home.

While we talk about Connection Sheets, drilling down, closing, and more, what we are really talking about is connecting. To be successful, you must know how to emotionally connect with people. As I have mentioned throughout this book, while you may think you are doing this, odds are you are not. Every system shared in this book is designed to further the connection you have with your prospects and their families:

❑ The Back-up Team: Eliminating mismanaged calls ensures that when people call, they feel important and your back-up team is crucial to first impressions.

❑ The Inquiry System: The Connection Sheets are designed to force you to focus on what's important to your prospects. It's natural to talk and share all about your community, but what people really want to know is, "What's in it for me?" Our inquiry system will make sure you talk less and listen more.

❑ The Visit Planning System: When people schedule appointments with you, that means they see value in taking their time to come see what you have to offer. The

Visit Planning Sheet and its components, such as engaging like-minded residents and wowing prospects are all designed to let people know we care, have listened, and understand that the things they shared and that you built into the visit are important. When people feel understood, it creates trust and further emotional connection.

❑ Follow-up System: Our thirty-day follow-up system is all about building trust and value early in the relationship. Each step is designed to provide information that will help with the decision process, stimulate further thought about what's important in the decision to move, and acclimate them with your community so the move will be easier.

❑ Closing: I spoke a lot about closing. Your job is not to sell people on your community or to convince them that it's a good fit. Your job is to get people excited to buy. When you can do that, you will be a sales master.

MINDSET

The final element is mindset. If you don't believe you can fill your building, you never will, no matter how great the systems. There is nothing more powerful than the mind. It will do exactly what you tell it to do. The problem is that many people never allow their minds to be still or to ponder what it is they really *want*, because they are so busy *doing*. Stop and think about what it is you want for your community or organization. From a sales standpoint, you have every tool needed within the pages of this book to reach 100% occupancy, and *Zero Lost Revenue Days*.

WHY IS THIS A REVOLUTIONARY APPROACH?

The definition of *revolutionary: introducing radical change.*

The sales side of our business is in dire need of radical change! While these systems may seem rudimentary to some who think they are already doing what I teach, yet are not, they represent the change that is needed to transform the way people perceive our services. The better experience people have when calling or visiting our communities, the more positive things they will have to say about it. What I do know is, we cannot continue to do business as usual. Those who keep doing what they have always done will keep getting what they've always gotten—mediocre results. Change is not optional, it's necessary for survival.

I am honored that you chose to read this book. I ask that you now choose to begin bringing change to your community or organization as a whole. Working within the senior housing industry has been the greatest honor in my professional life. Every day I am surrounded by people who want to make a difference, and that is empowering. I hope that through the words written on these pages, I can make a difference in your life and those you touch every day.

Thank you.

To contact Traci Bild, please e-mail her at TBild@BildandCo.com

To learn more about Bild and Company's Marketing, Training, or Research services, call 1.800.640.0688 or visit www.BildandCo.com.